Niche Publishing

Publish Profitably Every Time!

Gordon Burgett

Also written by Gordon Burgett

How to Plan a Great Second Life
Travel Writer's Guide
Niche Marketing for Writers, Speakers, and Entrepreneurs
Empire-Building by Writing and Speaking
Treasure and Scavenger Hunts
Sell and Resell Your Magazine Articles
How to Sell 75% of Your Freelance Writing
Publishing to Niche Markets
Self-Publishing to Tightly-Targeted Markets
How to Sell More Than 75% of Your Freelance Writing
Query Letters/Cover Letters: How They Sell Your Writing
Writer's Guide to Query Letters and Cover Letters
Speaking for Money (with Mike Frank)
Ten Sales from One Article Idea
The Query Book

Niche Publishing, by Gordon Burgett.

Published by Communication Unlimited
P.O. Box 845, Novato, CA 94948
(800) 563-1454 / FAX (415) 883-5707
www.nichepublishing.org

ISBN 978-0-979629525

TABLE OF CONTENTS

INTRODUCTION

The title of this book sounds like the true path to penury. Publishing is hard enough, but to niche markets? More work and greater risk to sell to fewer people?

You're in for a real surprise!

It may be the best kept secret in the book publishers' trove that big money, less risk, and a long-term, dependable income come from helping meet specific needs of reachable markets. In fact, within reason, the smaller the market, the better. Best yet, in this arena the small publisher can beat the giant at his own game every time!

The title of this book describes its contents precisely: how one publishes to niche markets. Yet the book does much more.

Beyond explaining the concept, it presents a system that will take you step-by-step through the process, and it shows as it tells with examples that you can follow or from which you can extrapolate to publish your own book and cull your own rewards.

Moreover, this process greatly reduces the risks and costs of publishing while increasing your profits and the certainty of them.

The book also talks about a philosophy, a way of sharing information.

It shows how, as a publisher, you can use your book as the core of a larger market penetration through which you can sell the same or related information more often and more widely.

That is, it suggests that, as important as your book is, the expertise that you display about its subject is more important still. That by sharing that expertise, through additional books or other information dissemination means, you can create an empire that could multiply your income mightily as you help others meet their needs.

But I'm getting ahead of myself. The next chapter begins the fleshing out of these promises.

Niche Publishing mostly talks about marketing, then writing, then expanding the marketing again, which is what all publishers do. And while the process focuses on books, the concept and many of the steps can usually be applied to any other means of information dissemination, such as articles, speeches, seminars, audio or video tapes, newsletters, or consulting.

I call it the "TCE process" because the three key elements are Targeting, Customizing, and Expanding. A section of the book is devoted to each element. But first I explain the concept in greater detail, show how standard publishing is inappropriate for almost all niche publishing, and how the alternate, the self-publishing path, is ideal for this purpose. Finally, a list of "other sources and guides" is included to help you apply the concept by creating your own book.

This book is about book writing and publishing because, of the many means, I know it best and I most want to share a new process about it with you. It is my 34th book. The first was sought by the major publisher in my field, Writer's Digest Books, but I decided to publish it myself. (They later included the second edition of that book, plus subsequent writing books, as top choices for their book club.) The decision to self-publish was the brightest thing I have done in decades. It gave me an opportunity to learn about the full spectrum of publishing from an independent yet involved perspective, which, in turn, led to the TCE process and this book.

The TCE process is neither a panacea nor publishing salvation. It simply will not work for some books, as I will explain. Yet it will work for many more, most of which would never be published by the standard houses and therefore would probably never be written and see print.

That is my greatest motivation for writing these pages. I am naive enough to believe that we can have a far better world on this earth and that one of the keys to its creation is knowledge shared as fully and widely as possible. Thought needs to be preserved; books are vital elements of that preservation. Our society puts a premium less on knowledge for its own sake than the sales value of that knowledge. Therefore, elements of information, particularly when its availability would be paid for by few, either remain unknown or never reach the book page. We—writers and potential readers—are the poorer for it.

The TCE process does not attempt to change the social norm but rather to expand the way that information can be made available and, yes, profitable, so it will be published in book form to far more people by many more writers. It simply makes books possible for more readers and for smaller readerships. That delights me immensely.

America—the world—is full of bright, articulate, insightful people who either have something to share or could have if they just knew that there is an easy-to-follow, self-directed path by which their words can reach readers—and for which they could be, at the same time, rewarded for having dared and worked to put them on paper.

Do I think that a real difference can be made by encouraging even more books in a world where too many books already go unread? You bet. Every new book writer is different and better for the act. And, yes, some of those books will contain bucketsful of trash. Many will follow well-trod paths, clichés flapping. But one or a dozen might change the world in a way never thought possible before its words were read. That book, or that dozen, might never have existed had a process like TCE not been suggested. So that too delights and motivates me.

Finally, an introduction is an opportunity to thank others who have made this book, and its thoughts, possible, though they aren't responsible for its contents, any errors, or folly it may contain.

My gratitude to Dan Poynter is such that this book is dedicated to him. Jim Comiskey has been a steady prod to better work and clearer thought. To the many unsung enablers in the grove of extended education who kept my debtors away and let me share this information through seminars while I pruned it for print, years of thanks. To my nephews—Doug Burgett, who keeps producing dandy covers for my books and those published by my company, and Brandon Carr, for technical assistance—love and pride. Finally, my gratitude to the many chapters of the National Speakers Association who heard these words, mercifully condensed, and made the kind comments that both kept a new idea afloat and convinced its aging skipper that it should be shared even more widely.

Actually, I'd have published this book even if nobody liked it because I think it offers a perspective and process that's needed, is perfectly in tune with today's technological state, and rewards the doer—the writer, producer, promoter, and seller called collectively the self-publisher—with the money, prestige, and promise he or she deserves.

But I have delayed you too long from seeing what TCE means and how it works if you do. So end the introduction; start the book!

DEDICATION

To Dan Poynter, whom I met by chance about the time my first book saw light. We were neighbors, the same age, and we kept running into each other at publishing events. From there a sort of Mutt-and-Jeff friendship developed and grew as we expanded into speaking. What most impresses me about Dan, beyond his knowledge, honesty, and solid experience in all facets of information dissemination, is his eagerness to share. Besides that, he's a nice guy.

ACKNOWLEDGEMENTS

Particular thanks to Sharon Rinderer, who made sense of the commas, semicolons, and spellings (if any errors escaped, the blame is mine) and, again, Doug Burgett, my "cover man," and by an odd coincidence Sharon's student a long time back a long way away. Barb, my wife, deserves huge gratitude for silently suffering as I plowed through what has to be every book writer's nightmare, a massive rewrite.

Chapter 1

The Premise

A niche is a unit that shares specific traits or behaviors in common. Proctologists are a niche. So are *baianos*, left-handed roofers, teachers, game show watchers, shepherds, and, yes, men or women.

My premise—provable again and again—is that, with reason, publishing to niches is far less risky, less expensive, faster, and likely far more profitable than publishing to just anybody (which is everybody). But there can't be too few of them (many thousands at least) or too many (the smaller and more cohesive the niche, the better).

Which says that there are two publishing worlds: (1) the usual, bookstore-fed broad and general market and (2) the much smaller, usually direct mail-driven niche market.

There's nothing particularly wrong with our cohorts who publish in (1). They have truths to share that they want in everybody's hands and theirs is just about the only way to get it done. But they usually pay a steep price. If they publish through the standard houses, they receive from 10-15% of the gross, get paid a couple of times a year, and they have almost no control over the look, title, or distribution of their creation. (Still, some do get rich and famous that way.) If they self-publish to everybody, that hill is steeper yet: they get all of the profits after all of the expenses are paid while they muscle the big houses all the way to be seen, read, and bought. Sheer tenacity and/or a killer book can sometimes win that race.

This book tells you how the second route will let you test your book before you write a chapter. If the tested like it, you create a product they are eager to buy, formfit it to their needs and desires, and sell it directly to those who are most benefited. That greatly reduces the risk, speeds up the process two- or threefold (or more), and lets you create a base from which you can sell many more related products. In fact, from that core information you can create an empire that will feed and fan you comfortably forever. (Oh yes, the product looks just like you plan it, has your title, and every time it is bought it further trumpets your name as an expert in its field.)

I'm making some assumptions. That you want to publish, you haven't got a ton of gold to start with, you are literate (or can find an editor friend who will make your words read right), you aren't adverse to earning reliable and substantial profits, and you have something to say (or can get something) that will make others (who can read) better, happier, richer, funnier, thinner, whatever it is they will buy to get or be.

For example, if you are the expert on widget burnishing but the process defies written explanation and your entire worldwide audience consists of seven scattered *aficionados* somewhere on the planet Earth, this book isn't for you.

But if you can tell others, say, how to sell widgets, if there are many thousands eager to increase (better, double) their widget-selling commissions, and if they are accessible, you're already on the path to profitable publishing. And if you can expand the selling information and it would interest other widget hawkers to learn more by other means (such as articles, audio CDs, videos, newsletters, or consulting), keep reading!

Why am I talking about those other things when what you really want to do is publish a book? Because what you are selling is none of those. You are selling information packaged as expertise, and those are simply some of the ways such information is sold. And if you can sell your information one way, like a book, you can usually sell it, with modifications, most of the other ways.

I will focus on one of those ways here: an ink-on-paper book. But if I totally isolated the book from the other means, a couple of things would happen. I would give you an incomplete, diluted view of the dynamics of information sharing akin to describing how to play baseball by focusing solely on bunting or running. And I'd be grossly derelict in showing you how, with only a fraction of additional effort, you could easily double your effectiveness and income.

Thus you will read about other means as well on these pages. Still, the overwhelming thrust of this text and its purpose is book-related, and with the exception of two short chapters and half of the third section, EXPANDING, books and publishing to niche markets are the core and substance of these pages. By understanding the book publication process you will be able to follow parallel steps for the other means, if they are applicable and you are interested.

Three more thoughts best shared now.

One, it's not enough just to have knowledge stored in your head. Even consultants have to share and adapt what they know for it to be profitable. They must convert what they know into applicable information upon which they or others can act.

The same for you. What makes information valuable to others is more than its existence. It must be available, understandable, and usable. How is that best done? By some information dissemination means, like a book.

The second point: you needn't be the foremost expert in the world to share information. In fact, you don't have to know much about your topic at all when you begin. The critical point is that the information you finally share is accurate, complete, and applicable. Not whether you spent a lifetime gathering it or a couple of no-nonsense months. The quality of your information will be judged by those who buy it. If it's good, they will want more of that good thing in other ways. If it's not, you've wasted your time, money, and energy. You simply don't know something that others will pay to know.

The third point: self-publishers usually write the book, then publish it. But that's not necessary. In this book I'm showing you how to publish a book—yours or others'. You needn't be the author. You will make more money if you write it too because you needn't pay royalties or some work-for-hire stipend. But a strong case can be made for finding other experts in a niche field, publishing their books, and following the "self-publishing" format, though I prefer "small press" to distinguish us from the big houses, whether we publish our own, others', or ours and others' books. In truth, it's all just publishing. (But the niche publishing path, mostly the order in which it progresses, is quite different.)

So far we've flirted with theory and fiddled with philosophy. Let's get to your book. Like, why not let some big-bucks publisher just take the written prose off your hands, send you fat royalty checks, and forget all this foolishness about doing the rest yourself? Stay tuned.

Chapter 2

Publishing as Usual:
The Standard Publisher

There are two key ways to publish a salable book, with some deviations. The conventional approach is to let a standard publisher do it for you. You write it and they produce, promote, and—you hope—sell it.

The second way is to do it yourself. You're in charge. You do it alone or, when necessary, hire others to do what they do better, quicker, or more economically, like a general contractor building a house. Except that here there is more than preparation and production. You must also promote your book, then sell it.

Most new writers are at best dimly aware of self-publishing. Others, aware, prefer to avoid or ignore it.

That's fine if you're writing a novel, a kid's book, or an encyclopedia. But if you're planning to write a book for a niche market, you cannot afford the luxury of such avoidance or the folly of such ignorance.

This chapter shows what standard publishers do. The next chapter discusses niche publishing. You must know the standard approach to understand how and why niche publishing is clearly better when writing to specifically identifiable clientele.

The Standard Approach

While there are many thousands of published book writers and surely hundreds of ways of progressing from a concept to the bookstore shelf to the remainder pile, many follow a process similar to this:

(1) The writer first finds a subject to write about, then researches to see
   (a) if another book currently exists, or soon will, about that subject;
   (b) if there is a market eager to buy the book;
   (c) which publishers produce books about that subject, and
   (d) which of those publishers should be approached in what order to produce their book.
(2) The writer prepares and submits a book proposal to the preferred publisher (or several) consisting of a query letter, an outline or table of contents, a synopsis (if necessary), a reference/resource sheet, and (sometimes) a sample chapter or two. (Some also involve agents at this point, though they are more often used for novels.)
(3) If at all interested, the publisher often sends the proposal and attachments to one or several advisors knowledgeable about the subject and replies to the writer after receiving responses from their advisors.
(4) The publisher tells the writer yes, no, or perhaps (indicating what changes would be necessary for acceptance). If the publisher wishes to see more of the book before giving a firm reply, the writer will usually be asked to submit sample chapters (often three).
(5) If the chapters are acceptable, the publisher will offer a contract which will include submission and payment schedules.
(6) Before offering the contract, the publisher will also conduct a marketing test, which may range from "asking around" to a full study.
(7) The writer researches and writes the book, then submits a draft.
(8) That manuscript is reviewed, edited, and returned to the writer for additions, alterations, and corrections.
(9) The writer submits a corrected draft.
(10) The publisher sends final galleys for the writer's approval, before printing.
(11) The book is printed. The publication process often takes 18 months after the corrected final draft is submitted.

(12) Sometimes the writer promotes the book, on radio or TV or by other means, after the book is offered for sale.

But all of that presumes the writer finds a publisher interested in the book. What kind of payment (and when) might that writer expect for a nonfiction trade book bought by a standard house today?

Typical nonfiction book contract payment rates/dates

(1) Average advance against royalties, first-time nonfiction book: $5,000.
(2) Royalty schedule: *cloth,* 10% of list = 1-4,999 copies
  12.5% = 5,000-9,999 copies
  15% = 10,000+
  trade paperback, 10% of list, all copies
  mass paperback, 6.5% of list, all copies
(3) No royalty on books given for reviews, promotions, etc.
(4) The advance against royalties paid in three installments:
  1/3 after the contract is accepted and returned,
  1/3 after the final corrected draft is received,
  1/3 after the book is released for sale.
(5) Royalty payment paid every six months after the advance against royalties has been met.
(6) Against potential returns, 15% of the royalties due are held until the following payment period.

That's about as good as it gets. Some publishers have higher paying plateaus, such as 10% to 15,000 copies sold, 12.5% to 50,000, and 15% from 50,001. Some stop royalties at 10% or 12.5% whatever the quantity sold. Some start the cloth payment at 8%. Many withhold more than 15% for returns each pay period. A few pay every three months; some pay annually. Almost all pay for the period ending three months prior to the actual payment date. (For example, the royalties received on June 1 were for sales up to March 1.) Some fudge on the accounting of the actual number of books sold. And a large percentage don't pay on list (or retail) at all, rather on net (which means about a 50% reduction in what the writer receives if the royalty percentages are the same).

Is it lucrative to publish a book through a major publisher?

It can be.

It can also be a foolish investment of time, energy, and creative skills, if profit is your motivation.

Let's say, arbitrarily, that it takes you 12 hours a week extra time, for six months, to compose your book on your computer, then edit it. That would be 288 hours (12 x 4 x 6) to get your book ready for print.

Further, let's say that a publisher accepts your book and prints 10,000 copies to sell at $19.95. Following the standard royalty schedule, you would be paid 10% of list for the first 5,000, then 12.5% for the remaining 5,000. Calculating the book's price at $20, you would earn a total of $22,500 in royalties.

If you divide $22,500 by 288 hours, you would be paid $78 an hour. Which, on the surface, isn't too bad. Particularly if you spend similar hours writing book after book—or spend the remaining hours earning a living. Alas, you don't receive that $22,500 all at once—or very quickly. And if any of these books are sold to a book club or at a discount greater than 50%, like to Amazon.com or through a wholesaler or distributor, your royalties could be as low as $10,000 total.

If the publisher gave you an advance against royalties of $5,000, that would likely have been paid in this way:

(1) $1,667 when the contract was signed, after having written several chapters—perhaps three months after the query go ahead;
(2) $1,667 when the final corrected draft was submitted—perhaps eight months to a year after the query go-ahead, and
(3) $1,666 when the book was released for sale—perhaps 18-24 months after the publisher first responded affirmatively to your query.

One of the greatest shocks to new book writers is how long it takes to actually receive their "big" money for a published book. Let's put our example in graph form and mercifully pay the full $22,500 to see when that money might be received. Remember, our example is for 10,000 cloth books at $19.95 (rounded off here to $20) with a $5,000 advance.

Pay-ment Month	Books Sold	Royalty %	Royalty Earned	15% Withheld	Previous Withheld	Amount Paid
24	3000	10%	$ 6000	$ 900	0	$ 100
30	2500	10% 2000	5250	788	900	5362
36	2000	12.5% 500	5000	750	788	5038
42	1200	12.5%	3000	450	750	3300
48	600	12.5%	1500	225	450	1725
54	400	12.5%	1000	150	225	1075
60	200	12.5%	500	75	150	575
66	100	12.5%	250	38	75	287
72	0	12.5%	0	0	38	38

If it took eleven months to write the final draft from the time you received a go-ahead to your query and another seven months for your book to see daylight, your book would first be offered for sale in the eighteenth month. Say that the publisher pays every six months and our chart starts with the first pay date, at the twenty-fourth month. And let's use a steadily declining rate of sales for simplicity, with 3,000 sold in the first six-month period.

That means that while your book was being written you received $1,667 at the signing, plus another $1,667 when the final corrected draft was submitted—a total of $3,332 the first year. In the second year you receive only the third part of the advance—$1,666—as the book was released. Or a total of $5,000 in two years.

Since the advance is just that, 10% of the first $50,000 earned (or 2,500 books sold in your case), you would receive only $100 at the first pay schedule because the first $5,000 of the $5,100 was paid in advance. Thus at the thirtieth month you receive your biggest check, $5,362.

The third year is the most lucrative: $10,400, with income in the subsequent three years $5,025, $1,650, and $325.

What is obvious is that publishing this way is less a livelihood than a sinecure, an income booster to augment another, more substantial source of income. So much for the yacht and hobnobbing with the literati.

Is there any way to get rich through the major houses? Sure, as many have. One way is to write material so good, so riveting, so widely sought, that despite the happenstance promotion (or, oddly, because of it) your name and words catch buyers' fancy.

That means writing novels that do better than what the best are already doing or something different, good, and liked. Or nonfiction books that hit the public appetite or need or curiosity at the right moment. The other way is to churn out more books, counting on volume to fill your coffers and create a cadre of readers eager for your next book. All of which means more sales, the perception of you as a moneymaker by your publisher, a fatter advance, and better promotion.

There are actually eight areas where you might increase or accelerate your profits with a nonfiction book: topic, market, quicker book preparation, quality, royalty payment, marketing, quicker book production, and follow-up.

Find a topic that's particularly "hot" or needed and you should sell more books, increasing your profits. Select a market looking for or needing a particular book and the same should occur. And prepare books as quickly as possible to increase your total income from all of your books in publication.

But the others won't help you much. Unless it is poor, book quality is marginal to your profits and is in the publisher's control anyway. You might shop for a better royalty schedule, but the field of differences is narrow. Publishers handle their own marketing and book production, so you can't change your own fate much there. And there is no follow-up by other means by most publishers. They sell your book and that's that. If you want to do anything more with that knowledge, good luck!

Will it sell?

Standard publishers have one overriding concern that writers cannot forget: to turn a profit and return a dividend to their stockholders. So their books, collectively, must make money. "Will it sell?" is the first and last question those truly in command must ask of each book. If it won't, you can bet your shoes it will be rejected or significantly changed.

Sales are the fruit and promotion is the fertilizer of publishing's true money trees. How those are done is where the TCE process and major publishers differ the most.

Major publishing houses aim their book sales at every literate American, plus any foreign rights they might grab along the way. So they can't fine tune topics too closely or they will eliminate huge chunks of potential buyers. They seek big topics. Broad subjects. Generic solutions that almost anybody can apply to his or her problems.

Which books thrive best with such a broad launching? Those that appeal to the greatest number of readers and those that appeal to the basest or most common interests. General books with wide readership.

Their marketing must be done on an equally grand scale, usually through bookstores, to have the books available for purchase when the promotion stimulates the buyer's urge. Libraries must also be convinced of widespread reader interest so the book will be bought for their collections. As must textbook buyers, and teachers, for use in classrooms nationwide.

That process is appropriate for mass selling of books. Novels of mayhem, murder, or madness, for example, may appeal to a wide spectrum of readers, particularly if they touch all three. A generic *How to Lose Weight* or *How to Reduce Your Income Taxes by 50%* will find favor in many households.

But how does the major publisher market *Secretaries: How to Lose Weight* or *Dentists: How to Reduce Your Malpractice Insurance Premiums 50%*? Given a choice between generic books and the more limited markets, major houses pick generic books every time, despite the fact that there were 3,522,000 secretaries (and administrative assistants) and 167,000 practicing dentists in the United States in 2004—and even more today.

Let's pursue the book for dentists and malpractice insurance for a moment. Presume that you know how to reduce malpractice insurance, are certain that every dentist would be interested, and you think that a book would be the best way to share this information widely and quickly.

You're in for a substantial surprise if you think that a standard book publisher will accept that book! Their disinterest has little to do with the worth of the idea, your credentials, or how well you write. You won't get a nibble for one very basic reason: the market is too small for the bigger houses to work.

Specific targets require marketing they don't do. The larger houses, with very few exceptions, produce books to be sold through distributors to bookstores, chains, schools, libraries, and other mass volume outlets, brick or digital. And dentists, other than by chance, do not buy books related to dentistry in mall bookstores or at the supermarket. They buy them from mailed fliers or from the Web, through association journals and newsletters, from display ads in dental-related magazines, at conventions, through reviews in their publications, and by word-of-mouth. So almost all standard publishers will reject your query since they didn't get big by producing books that sell small.

Yet some do work specialty markets, and your book may be just what they are seeking. Beware. An example from a student I recently taught shows why. He proposed a book about word processing to a major publisher selling by direct mail to the business world (as well as through bookstores). They were interested and suggested a 700-page how-to text in workbook form that they would sell for $80. He would receive an advance of $4,000-6,000 against royalties of 5% of the list price, or $4 for every $80 item sold. Which means, if his advance was $5,000, he wouldn't get another cent until the publisher had made $100,000. And for the author to earn $50,000 in profit the publisher would have to reap $1,000,000! (He said no.)

The TCE process that this book outlines would have you earn at least half of that million dollars as profit—or ten times, at least, what you would earn from a standard publisher generous enough even to be interested in selling your information!

So standard publishers aren't the way to sell information to niche markets.

The final insult...

Even if a standard publisher accepts your book and brings it to print, he will probably abandon it if it doesn't sell well and quickly. At the risk of generalizing to make a point, promotion at many of the larger publishing houses follows the "flaming arrow" approach. The house launches 20 or 100 books at once, shooting all of their arrows skyward. They have told the public in advance to watch for certain books, those bearing the names of their popular authors, their proven moneymakers. The publisher watches the rest, and if one or another of the new arrows catches fire when it lands, it gets fanned. That is, the publisher blows up instant promotion and prints more copies to meet the demand, which is increased by the new promotion. After working them for obvious sales and trying to earn back at least the production costs and paid advance, the other books are left to quietly die.

There's nothing evil or particularly absurd about the way standard publishers run their business given their large-scale orientation, size, and relative isolation from the book buyer. But there's nothing to commend it for a book to a niche market either.

There's simply a better way

If you're eager to share specific information with an identified, niche market, and, yes, you too would like to earn a handsome profit like the standard publishers, and, moreover, you'd like much more of it and sooner, publishing houses are the wrong venue for your book.

That the major houses opt for broad markets is a huge blessing for you. It's an entrepreneur's dream! From either the book to secretaries or dentists—which are but two examples from thousands of other ideas and titles—you could earn 50% profit or more from each book (not 6-15%), then double that again by other means, at the same time creating an empire of lifetime earnings.

Even if major publishers were interested in limited market books, publishing through them would at best reward you with small royalties, slow payments, and their generally fitful marketing practices. And they would do nothing to promote the follow-up or to enhance your empire. Which is where the TCE process functions best.

With TCE you start with a market, figure out what it needs, write a book that meets that need, produce the book yourself (contracting out what others do better), sell directly to your chosen market, expand the ways you share that information by either other information means or more books, and use all of the knowledge gained and products developed to create an on-going empire.

In the next chapter we will see how publishing the TCE way does far better what standard publishers don't do well at all: getting your niche book to all of your markets quickly and very profitably.

Chapter 3

AN ALTERNATIVE: A BOOK SPECIFICALLY PUBLISHED TO NICHE MARKETS

We said at the beginning of the last chapter that there are two ways to publish a salable book: through a standard publisher or by doing it yourself.

That's not quite true. There are really three key ways to get a book published, and you do two of them yourself. They differ by how the book will be marketed and, to a lesser degree, by the organizational steps leading up to that marketing.

We've discussed the first method, standard publishing, at least sufficiently to see that it isn't the preferred path for niche books.

The second method draws from both camps. It is publishing with standard marketing. Which means that the publisher produces the book but then tries to sell it by using standard publishing methods.

The third method is publishing the TCE way.

The second and third methods share the same publishing developmental stages of preparation, production, and promotion. They are virtually identical at the production stage, and thus the best how-to book about publishing at this level, Dan Poynter's *Self-Publishing Manual*, is an excellent guide concerning a book's production and much of its preparation.

The biggest difference lies in promotion.

The marketing thrust of the Poynter book envisions a successful self-publisher as a person who produces his or her own book and markets it well and widely by using the same basic selling techniques as larger, standard publishers, though with more persistence and some modification. They allow for additional creativity and tailoring to a specific market but see that as secondary. Most sales would come through bookstores (walk-in and digital), distributors, libraries, and chains. Good reviews would draw additional sales. Selling to niche markets is poorly addressed, as is direct marketing by mail.

The TCE process—which, again, stands for targeted, customized, and expanded—requires a much different approach to marketing for the simple reason that the book will rarely, if ever, be bought at bookstores or chains. Rather, it is written specifically—customized to a clearly defined market—and is sold directly to the people in that market, primarily by mail or the Internet, secondarily by more general techniques such as reviews in appropriate journals or newsletters, display ads in those same vehicles, catalogs or card decks directed to that market, a booth at regional meetings or the convention, articles that marketfolk would read, and other means mentioned by Poynter or also explained in John Kremer's *1001 Ways to Market Your Book*.

The order of activity and planning is different too. The reader isn't a vague half-form dimly floating in space to whom the book is generally written. In the TCE process, the reader is a buyer from a clearly-defined and understood market, a person who will purchase the book for a very precise reason and who expects its contents to do very specific things. So the definition of that reader/buyer and what he or she will (or will not) buy precedes the writing. In fact, before a word of text goes on paper the writer knows the selling plugs in the sales cover letter that will make the buyer rush to order the book!

There's more. Where standard publishers stop at book production and self-publishing texts hint at topic life after print, the "E" of the TCE process stands for "expanded," or the greater use of the information being sold, as is or modified, by other means.

Where the TCE process also differs is by integrating this expansion by other information dissemination means early into the process. It identifies all of the ways by which that information can be sold, designs a developmental path, and uses the book's preparation as a source and spur to create other means before, during, and after the book appears in final form. It also helps structure the book so that it can serve as a valuable on-going information source for other means. One example would be the creation and implementation of a seminar for which the book is a vital workbook and take-home tool.

In standard and conventional publishing, money flows as long as the book is bought, and when that last copy goes, income stops. Not so the TCE way.

Why should you publish the TCE way?

Because you can get your words in print, earn far more money, greatly reduce the time it takes to put those words in published book form, control the contents and appearance of your book, direct the ways by which your information and book are sold, and integrate into and around your book the other means by which that same, similar, or subsequent information can also be sold.

Some specifics, in contrast to following the standard publishing model just discussed:

(1) You needn't convince any other publisher that your ideas and words are worth their time, energy, and investment so they will develop your book. That can save you months or years.
(2) You can set your own pace for the book's preparation, production, and promotion.
(3) Your profit per book may well exceed 60-65%, and should top 50%. That money can also be yours the moment payment is received, without a reserve for returns.
(4) You can determine how many books to print, when, and how they will be bound or customized for market needs.
(5) You won't be abandoned by another publisher if your book doesn't sell quickly and well—unless you give up on yourself
(6) You are in control of promotion and sales, from inception to remaindering.

What's the catch?

Writing a book is hard, exacting work. Publishing it is three times harder and continues until that last copy is bought, burned, or donated. If you earn five or ten times as much by publishing it yourself, you earn every cent. That's risk money because it's your capital that pays for preparation, production, and promotion. Every trip to the library, every book printed and shrinkwrapped, every shipping invoice or flyer comes from your coffers—most of it long before a dime returns.

What hurts most is the disdain in which you will be held for having invested dearly in putting your ideas and words in print, for publishing your book yourself. Self-publishing both in the trade and outside is still held in low esteem. The unknowing usually assume that you couldn't get another publisher to accept your book so you had no other choice! (Which, incidentally, may be true but speaks as much to the weaknesses of other publishers as to your ideas and writing abilities.)

It's labyrinthine and perilous too. Plenty of steps to follow, one thing before another, pitfalls, nobody to pull you through and shout praises or point before you step off some financial cliff.

Well, who promised it would be fun? (But it is, usually.) Who guaranteed you utter and certain success? (That can happen nonetheless.) And anyway, what worth doing doesn't have a learning curve and pitfalls and financial cliffs and the great, singular satisfaction of seeing the results that also help others build a better world?

Life's a game, and so is publishing. As serious a game as you want to make it. The prize can be a bag of bullion and your words in print for all time. Want to play? Our game is called TCE and it requires 14 steps. Step one is next!

TARGETING

The "T" of TCE means "Targeted"

To target in this context is to find a group of potential book buyers with a need that you want to help them solve, then identify that need, and finally to qualify the group to see that there are enough of them, they are accessible by mail, and they have the desire and money to buy your book to help meet their need. You do this, in part, to reap the bountiful rewards that niche publishing, well done, can bring.

It all starts here. If you target well, customizing and expanding, the "C" and "E" of TCE, follow.

"An expert is a person who has made
all the mistakes that can be made
in a very narrow field."

Niels Bohr (1885-1962)

Chapter 4

FINDING, DEFINING, AND QUALIFYING THE TARGET MARKET

"Targeted" means knowing specifically who will buy your book, why, how much they will pay (or won't), how they would hear about your tome, and what your promotion must say to get them to make that purchase.

In other words, you don't write a word until you've answered those questions. Then every word you do write is written directly to that market and fulfills each and every promise made in the promotion. If you are writing a book telling bank tellers how to become bank presidents, the book will outline, then detail, precisely how that rise can be made and how the reader can follow the advice. Your book will be written to ambitious bank tellers, period. It seemed in years past there were millions of them—but now there are about 425,000.

So you must first pick a group of people to write to.

That group of people is your market. Niche books are written to specific people, to clearly identifiable "somebodies." The first step is finding the right target, then defining and qualifying it.

Writing to "anybody" won't do if you plan to publish your own book, have limitations on your budget, and hope to receive a bountiful profit soon. Save the broad markets for other publishers who have the money and, sometimes, the moxie to make them work.

Rather, think small and tight. Pick a target for your book that is definable and accessible and has a need that it wants to meet plus the funds and desire to buy a book to do so. If that's not enough, there must also be a sufficient number of those somebodies eager and able to buy your book.

Many thousands of just such markets exist. There is a shockingly large number of somebodies joined together by like interests and needs who will buy a book to meet them. Best yet, they aren't very hard to find.

Let's amplify and restate the qualifications for a TCE target market, to better serve as a guide. To be an acceptable TCE market, a group of people must:

(1) **share something in common**, such as a profession (doctors, placement directors, welders), job title (fulfillment packers, food vendors, janitors), or experience (Korean War veterans, former Chicago Cubs);

(2) **appear on** an accessible, affordable, and current or "clean" **mailing list**;

(3) **share a pressing need** or needs;

(4) **have both a sufficient desire and the income** to seek and afford information about meeting that need, and

(5) **be sufficiently numerous** to make provision of the information profitable to the provider.

All five are important, and each must be interpreted in terms of the best interests of publishing your book. In (1), for example, not all who share a common interest will qualify. If the interest they share is their fierce individualism, that would likely preclude each from buying a book that others bought, at least for that reason. If what binds them together is a hatred of books, the group is even less promising for your purposes.

The second qualification comes from the need to make the targeted market aware of the book's existence and desirability. You simply must know who and where the buyers are. By extension, since that market is likely to be scattered, they will most likely be contacted promotionally by mail. Therefore a current mailing list is doubly important. Which excludes people without reasonably fixed addresses, like transients or the homeless, as good markets for TCE books, though they indeed share something vital in common and have a pressing need.

Income is also a factor, as noted in qualification four. The need your book meets must, in the minds of the market, be worth the cost of that book. And the buyers must have sufficient capital to make that purchase. However worthy the advice or information, it will not be bought by the utterly destitute.

And there simply must be enough people in the market able and eager to buy your book to make its preparation and production worthwhile.

To speak in more specific terms for the remainder of this text, let's say that you plan to earn $50,000 profit from your first niche book. Plus you plan to earn that much again by other means. Which doesn't limit you to $50,000 from either source, or $100,000 in total, but simply gives us firm numbers to work with right now.

How many people must there be in your target market to earn that $50,000 book profit? Say that it costs you $4,000 to produce the book. Your market would need only 18 people—if every one of them bought a copy and paid $3,000 for it!

Alas, most markets don't buy at a 100% ratio nor will they pay $3,000 a copy. In fact, most buyers start hedging when a book costs above $15, think very long at $25, and are in full retreat at $50—significantly short of $3,000. Since promotional costs rise in close ratio to the number in the market to be contacted, a profit of $50,000 is far more likely to require a market that numbers from 30,000 to 75,000.

Let's add some more variables to your $50,000 book profit goal, to establish a base that we can use for calculations for the rest of this text. Let's say that (1) you are offering the only book that meets the need, (2) your book will cost $20 (though you will actually sell it for $19.95 because a buyer will mentally justify spending "$19 and change" more easily than $20), (3) you will sell the book directly to the buyer, eliminating handlers' discounts, (4) the buyer will pay the postage and tax as part of the purchase price add-on, (5) it will cost you 50% of the selling price to produce, promote, and market your book, and (6) you will sell the book to 10% of your targeted market. Given those conditions, to reap a $50,000 profit your targeted market must have 50,000 buyers.

How could you reduce that number? You could cut it in half by doubling the book price—or by selling to 20% instead of 10% of your targeted market. If you did both you would need a target market of only 12,500! Another obvious way would be to reduce production, promotion, and marketing costs, which are very high at 50%. But the very best way to hit the optimum profit level is to strike right at the heart of the market's greatest need(s) and make your book irresistible at every step.

Let me pose an additional thought now, the value of which will become more evident as this book progresses. Many markets will meet all five qualifications, yet among them some markets will yield one book and little else while others will produce enough riches to last a lifetime. Three characteristics are found in the latter: continual growth of the market, a quick turnover of its members, and/or a steady development of products to satisfy new needs.

Must you be a member of a group or market to write about it?

No, but the process will probably be quicker and more certain if you do share at least some of the same interests.

Why? Because you will have a better, more intimate sense of the group's problems and needs, you will have a better understanding of its buying practices and preferences, you may have access to the group's leaders or others more knowledgeable about the topic of your book, and you may have preferred access to the group's newsletter, mailing list, convention or meeting plans, and other "inside" information.

That you are not a member can be partially offset by careful research, joining the group and getting quickly integrated into its activities, co-authoring with a member or a person well-informed of its activities, and/or having a member or well-informed person accessible with whom you can frequently verify the validity of your book's content.

How can you check on the existence and size of accessible markets?

Since a mailing list is essential and its size is a key determinant to market appropriateness, perhaps the best source would be directories or catalogs of mailing lists. Available in many of the larger libraries is a publication called *Direct Marketing List Source* published by Standard Rate and Data Services. It used to be easy to find and it was full of information. An SRDS directory now leads you to thousands of list brokers; it used to tell you the list's rental or purchase cost, forms in which the list could be provided, ways it could be sub-divided, how long it took for the list to be sent, restrictions on its use, and other information.

Now you must go to the brokers to get that information at no cost. The brokers will tell you the total number of names currently listed, and sometimes by area or category.

You can also use your mailing list house to find lists for you, as I explain later.

What kinds of groups/professions have 50,000+ listed?

The sample list that follows gives an idea of the kinds of markets available for a TCE book that have more than 50,000 names listed.

> physician assistants – 70,000
> chiropractors – 73,000
> pest control workers – 75,000
> refuse and recyclable material collectors – 81,000
> tax preparers – 88,000
> logging workers – 92,000
> database administrators – 94,000
> travel agents – 95,000
> insurance underwriters – 98,000

Each of those categories needs specific, tightly-targeted niche books. Yet those are some of the smallest groups listed in the "Employed Civilians by Occupation, 2004" in the *Statistical Abstract of the United States 2006: The National Data Book* (see pages 401-4). Only 15% of the 287 categories had fewer than 100,000 employees. Here's a quick sampling of some larger groups:

aircraft pilots and flight engineers – 118,000
bakers —188,000
pharmacists – 233,000
bank tellers – 424,000
education administrators – 757,000
electricians – 781,000
CEOs – 1,680,000

If your targeted field includes associations, check the *Encyclopedia of Associations* available at most libraries. It can help in two ways: the current membership and the names of the publications the association produces. Often you may rent both the membership list and the publication subscriber list, though sometimes they are for members only. It would make little sense to rent both if the magazine is distributed exclusively to members. The best situation for you is when the publication accepts outside subscriptions, is widely bought by those in the field, is sent to all members, lists every recipient, and its list can be rented by the public.

SRDS also publishes other books including the *Newspaper Advertising Source, Business Publication Advertising Source,* and *Consumer Magazine Advertising Source,* which list other publications, with circulation statistics, which those in the targeted field might read in a library. A quick cross-check with the SRDS mailing list directory or a letter or call to the publication itself will reveal whether the subscription list is rentable.

Often the fastest way to identify those most interested in a topic is to find the most highly respected newsletter in the field. How do you test respect? Probably by asking those in the target field receiving all available publications. To find addresses and pertinent information about the many newsletters now available, see the current Thomson Gale publication, *Newsletters in Print*.

And don't forget an obvious source of general data: the many almanacs in your library, such as *The World Almanac* and *The World Factbook.*

The purpose of this step? To find, define, and qualify your book's target market. You have to write your book to a specific collective somebody—the right somebody. In the following chapter we will further qualify that market by its need.

**"Believe one who has proved it.
Believe an expert."**

Virgil (70-19 BC)

Chapter 5

FINDING AND DEFINING
A SPECIFIC MARKET NEED

Once you've found a target market to write to, you need a subject, or topic, to write about!

Not all subjects are equal. To find the right subject you must ask, "Why would people in my target market buy my book?"

Given a thousand other things they could buy with their money, and as many other ways they could use their energy rather than studying your words, why would they suffer the expense and make the effort to read what you have written?

Because to do so would bring them benefit or benefits. Two kinds of benefits are most likely to get them to respond: one that meets a pressing need or one that solves a critical problem.

The benefits can be personal, job- or family-related, or linked to peers or friends. The strongest motivations are achievement, advancement, acquisition, or not losing what one already has. And the rewards one can receive from meeting a need or solving a problem? Money, promotion, esteem, respect, happiness, survival, security, order, immortality, leisure, the opportunity to use one's abilities to the fullest, ...

Logically, then, the greater the need, the more likely people will want it met. And if the solution to that need comes in book form, the greater the likelihood that they will buy the book. So your TCE success is directly related to finding that crucial need or solution, meeting or solving it on your pages, and telling people with that need that your book exists to help them solve it.

Matching that need to your target market

Every target market has a dozen needs, maybe hundreds, or thousands, that it would pay to help meet. For example, some of those needs might concern process or procedure. Those in the market know what must be done but need help doing it or doing it better. The needs are problems seeking solution. You must find those needs your market most wants met or those problems it most desperately wants to solve.

It makes no sense writing a book full of information that nobody wants. Or that nobody will pay much, if anything, to know. Rather, you want to provide eager buyers with information that is so vital, so critical they would be fools not to want it at any reasonable price. And since your plan is to realize a just profit from providing needed information, finding precisely the right subject meets both of your criteria.

Let me suggest two approaches to help you ferret out from the hundreds of possible needs or solutions of your target market the one best suited for your book.

One way to find your subject

The first approach presumes an intimate knowledge of the target market and suggests eleven steps to bring the best subject(s) to the surface.

(1) Form a mental picture of a typical person from your target market. Make a list of every problem that person would encounter during an average day that might also be experienced by others from that market. Add special problems from atypical days. Then add every activity, event, or thing that would create stress or frustration in any person from that target market.

(2) Look at that person's total life. How could that life be improved? What problems do others from that target market share? What solutions would help all? What needs must be resolved?

(3) What dreams does your person have? What hopes? How could those be realized? Which of those dreams do all in that market share? Which are the most important? Which, if resolved for one, would be resolved for all?

(4) Why would your typical person from the target market buy your book? To do a better job? To make more money? To improve their family life? To make a more lasting contribution to society?

(5) Review the answers to the questions just asked and list a dozen topics, or needs, that your typical person from that niche market would buy a book to help meet. Then rearrange that list by urgency or importance of topic, with the most critical first.

(6) Place next to each of those topics a percentage of people in the target market who would see that topic as critical and would likely buy a book about it. Consider the second factor in estimating that percentage: would each person buy their own book or, if bought by one, would the book be widely shared? Or would the book be bought by a group of people, to be shared?

(7) If the price of the book were $20, how would that affect the number of buyers? Adjust possible prices and the likely percentage of your buyers accordingly.

(8) Books don't write and produce themselves, nor is that done instantly. Figure a minimum of two months, with six to ten a more realistic release date from the inception of the idea (particularly for the first publication). How will this alter the order of your list? Which topics won't be critical at that time? Which might be even more urgent?

(9) Now reorder your list. The ideal topic is one desperately desired by every member of your target market. Better yet, one that will be even more desired at the time of publication. The need that your book helps meet should be central to the life of its buyer. Every member would not only pay $20 for the book, each would want his or her own copy. And would want even more help in the field beyond that book.

(10) Sadly, few books are so fervently awaited or so totally wanted. List the books closest to that ideal first, giving particularly high value to the number of potential buyers.

(11) Now evaluate each book by asking whether it could in fact be written. Is there sufficient information to fill 100-250+ pages?

Would the contents be worth far more than the $20 you might charge? Would the buyer receive a personal advantage or benefit from knowing that book's contents?

A second and complementary way

The second approach is more likely to be used by an outsider or one with more casual, or less intimate, knowledge of the target market, though it is an excellent additional exercise for those following the 11-step system just suggested.

Its purpose, again, is to find a subject that everyone in the target market wants to know or know more about.

(1) Ask those in the market exactly what they desperately want or need to know more about!
(2) See which market-related needs or problems are mentioned in recent, appropriate professional/trade journals and trade magazines, ezines, or blogs.
(3) Check newspaper indexes to see what is new, changing, or projected for the future of the target market and about which information would be wanted.
(4) Google to find other, recent niched articles about your topic.
(5) See what already exists (or soon will) among the books directed to your market, to see what is needed, what should be updated, and what must be redone. Check the library stacks and digital holding lists, plus the current *Subject Guide to Books in Print*, *Books in Print*, and *Forthcoming Books*.

The result?

The best possible subject for your TCE book, several subjects for several books (from which the best first book might be chosen), several subjects that could be combined into a super first book, or a wealth of information that could be shared by many means beyond a first book—after that is written and sold!

If you fail to find a subject, look again. There is virtually no target market without a dozen screaming needs begging to be met.

CUSTOMIZING

The "C" of TCE means "Customized"

In the "T" of the TCE process you "targeted" your market, then you found one or several needs of that market.

Now, in the "C" you are going to "customize" your information to meet that specific need for that particular market. Here you will tailor-fit your book, every stitch for a purpose, custom-sewn to one person or one group. Your book will be written in their language. It will look like books they buy. It will be bound and decorated and illustrated specifically to their tastes. Most important, your book will do one thing and do it fully: meet that critical need or solve that pressing problem. And it will do it solely with that buyer in mind.

The section chapters that follow talk about customizing your book specifically to your niche market.

"It's not enough to create magic.
You have to create a price for magic, too.
You have to create rules."

Eric A. Burns (1947-   )

Chapter 6

MEETING THAT NEED THROUGH A BOOK: CHECKING, MEASURING, AND FITTING

Having found and defined a specific need that you can meet or a solution you can provide in your book, it's imperative to do three more things: (1) see if that need can be, or soon will be able to be, met by someone else's book, or several; (2) develop a purpose statement, a working question, and all necessary secondary questions to serve as the book's basic organizational structure, and (3) determine whether there is sufficient material to fill a book's pages.

In other words, next is the necessary checking, measuring, and fitting to see whether a book is the appropriate means for sharing your information. As important, can it be prepared the TCE way? And will it bring you your desired profits?

What if a book isn't the proper or best way? Maybe a different information dissemination means is. We'll discuss that in the next chapter. Best you know now before investing more time, effort, and money in a book that isn't, to you, fully worth writing!

Is this need being met by one or many other books?

Why write a book that already exists, or soon will? Fortunately, in the computer age you needn't guess. Just dig out the facts. The results of your research will pay you handsomely since what you find you can use again and again in your TCE quest.

First, go to your library and find your subject in the digital holdings catalog. List every sub-category by which related information is also found. (Article indexes can help show related sub-categories.) Armed with the topic heading and related headings where you might also find valuable material, begin your resource compilation. You are actually seeking two kinds of information: (1) that which directly addresses the need you wish to help meet through your book, and (2) related information about that need and similar needs.

A quick example of how the latter might be used, beyond indicating source books for reference during your later research? Let's say that your intent is to write a book called *How to Create a Better School.* But when you check the library you find many good, general books that explain just that. Yet none specifically addresses particular kinds or levels of school. A possible result? Your new book might be called *How to Build a Better Middle School* or *How to Design a Perfect School for the Gifted.*

Here are some steps to take to see if the need has already been adequately covered, what other books exist about it in print (or soon will), what your book may have to contain to be competitive or sufficiently comprehensive, and what other books about closely related topics are available.

(1) You have a choice of having a comprehensive computer search conducted by an outside source or you can do it yourself. Librarians at major universities often know who does these best, graduate students (especially in library sciences) often moonlight doing this research, or you can use google.com to find commercial sources. You are looking for all key titles of books plus the most useful books, articles, or other related means in the library or on the Internet. To keep the cost rea-

sonable and the results useful, work closely with the researcher first to identify precisely what information you want and by which categories it can be found.

(2) If you do this yourself, or to supplement the outside computer search, check the following library sources for books about your subject: the holdings catalog (manual or computerized, including microfiche and microfilm listings), the stacks themselves to find books either unlisted or poorly titled (for your purposes), the current *Subject Guide to Books in Print* (which lists the books published in the past few years, each with the publisher's name and address), the current *Forthcoming Books*, (which lists books that will be released in the coming six months, with a short description of each and the publisher from which they can be purchased), any Library of Congress subject index listing that is available, plus, of course, the bibliographies of those books found. On the long shot, you might see if any booklets or pamphlets are hiding in a vertical index or file—ask the librarian.

(3) Divide the books found into two groups: (a) those in direct competition with your book, that either meet the need you wish to meet or are close enough in theme that a person in your target market may buy them instead of your book, and (b) those about related or similar subjects that aren't directly competitive but which you will want to consult for research.

(4) For the second group, prepare an annotated bibliography from the information they list or mention. List the author or editor, full title, publisher, date of publication, and where you can find the book cited for later consultation (if you know). Add to that anything you know or can deduce about that book's contents as it relates to your topic.

(5) For the first group, those which compete with your book, you need to know far more. Here you must study both content and form to see the market standard, to serve as a guide to what a comprehensive book about this topic contains, and to see what your book needs. (If the competition isn't as good as it might be or as comprehensive as it should be, that can provide you with an excellent marketing advantage. Alas, you must study the rest to know that.) This is what you need to know about every book in this primary group:

(a) author(s) or editor(s)

(b) other books written by the same author(s) or editor(s)

(c) full title (including sub-title[s])

(d) publisher (with address)

(e) date of publication

(f) date of copyright and by whom

(g) number of editions or printings and the dates of each

(h) whether the book is part of a series; if so, information about the series, its theme, items (a)-(c) and (e)-(g) above about each book

(i) form of binding or publication of all forms of this book: cloth, paper, spiral, digital, audio CD, etc.

(j) cost of each of the books in (i)

(k) number of pages; number in each chapter or section

(l) why the book was written—check the introduction or first chapter where the purpose statement or working question often appears; more on these later in this chapter

(m) kinds and number of illustrations used and the sources of each, where identified

(n) number and kind of charts, graphs, maps, etc. and whether each was prepared for this book or is a reprint from another source. If the latter, what source?

(o) number and kind of how-to guides

(p) whether the book is designed for classroom use. If so, explain. For example, does it contain a summary and exercises after each chapter?

(q) Does it contain a foreword? Who wrote it?

(r) Are there testimonials in the book? Where? By whom?

(s) Are other products sold through the book? What are they? How are they sold? Is a price list printed? Where does it appear? Describe each of the products in detail.

(t) Does the book mention future editions or books about this or a related topic? Give full details.

(u) Describe the bibliography; does it list books only? Articles? Other information sources? What is the most recent item listed? How many items are listed?

(v) Does it include a glossary? Table of contents? Index? List of illustrations? Dedication? Introduction?

(w) Describe the appendix, if any. What is listed? How many pages long is it?

(x) Is the book current? Out-of-date? Incomplete? Misdirecting? Evaluate the book in these and any other terms that will identify its position in the body of literature about this field.

(y) Where was this book reviewed? What did reviewers say about it? In retrospect, are they accurate?

By studying other books designed and published to meet the need in detail, you can see how your book must differ (if at all) to compete profitably. Even if other available publications don't directly address the same need, a close review of their structure and content will provide a model to be followed, modified, or ignored. Some questions that such a review might provoke are:

(1) How can you slant or direct your focus to create a new, different, better, more desirable book? Or is any or all of that necessary? Said in a different way, how can you make your book, among the others now or soon to be available, sufficiently unique and wanted to be bought by at least 10% of the target market at $20 a copy?

(2) How could this book be better tied to the target market? What is unavailable—at all, at this level, in this way—to the desired buyer that this book might provide? How could the book's unique features be made known to those who might buy it?

(3) How could you increase the perceived value of the book? A foreword by a well-known expert in the field? A co-author with wider recognition? More or different how-to guides and checklists? A companion workbook? Testimonials on the front or back cover, or both?

(4) What other means of information dissemination might you use to increase your sharing of this information while also increasing your profits?

Developing the organizational structure of your book

In-depth research about competition and other, related resources is crucial to finding your book's unique core and its selling "hook."

Still, there's something even more important to finding that unique core. You must know precisely what you hope to achieve with your book. What is its purpose?

So the next steps explain how to develop a purpose statement, a working question, and all the secondary questions necessary to creating your book's basic organizational structure.

A purpose statement

This is as uncomplicated as it sounds. Explain, in one sentence, the purpose of your proposed book. "The purpose of my book is ..." But one sentence only. If you need two or three, you still don't know what your book will be about.

It may be uncomplicated but it isn't always easy to zero in that tightly. Still, it must be done, and the earlier the better. It simplifies the research and writing task by providing you a measuring tool as you work.

Woe to the writer who heads into the word jungle to write a book, thinking to research and write the definitive study of the gnat, only to discover that what he really wants to tell is how to catch a hippo. He's in the wrong woods with the wrong tools for the wrong reason, wasting too much time reporting very wrong facts.

A working question

Now rewrite that one-sentence statement into a working question. From "The purpose of this book is to explain how to catch a hippopotamus," you would write "How does one catch a hippopotamus?"

Why? Because your book answers that question. By doing so it achieves its purpose. If it doesn't, why bother? Your reader expects to find out how to catch a hippo from the title and everything that your promotion promises. Anything less angers the buyer, creates true distress for you, and probably delights hippos.

The working question is the plumb line that everything included in the book must touch. It is the gauge by which items are included, trimmed, stretched, or deleted. Any material that doesn't tell how to catch a hippo, directly or indirectly, is material for somebody else's book—or yours later when you write another book that it does address.

Secondary questions

Secondary questions flow from the primary question. They usually begun with "who, what, why, where, when, or how"—the working tools of journalists.

> "Where might you catch a hippo?"
> "How is it done?"
> "When?"
> "What tools would you need?"
> "Who could do it? What skills would it require?"
> "Why would you even want to try?"

Most writers can think of 30 or 40 secondary questions that virtually ask themselves once the working question is posed. To fully understand the answer to the working question, it's necessary to understand the secondary questions.

So write out every such question that comes to mind. Spend time here. Put them all down. And then rearrange the questions in some sensible order. If your book is historical in theme, list the questions chronologically. If its theme is how to catch a hippo, consider a developmental order. If it's a how-to action book based on others' experiences, perhaps list case studies in either a chronological or developmental format. You figure out what works best to achieve your purpose.

What comes from defining a purpose statement, putting it in working question form, writing down the secondary questions that must be answered to fully respond to the working question, then putting those secondary questions in some sensible order? A book outline. Not in marble, not definitive with its parts unalterable, but nonetheless a solid book outline that will give structure and a spine to all that follows.

Usually the secondary questions, reduced to key words, become chapter headings. And the words that answer those secondary questions become the contents of that chapter. They provide the substance, ideas, dreams, humor, and expression of the book.

Each chapter answers its own secondary question. Cumulatively, the chapters answer the working question, and, by doing so, your purpose, expressed in the purpose statement, is achieved.

That achievement, in terms of your book, is the reason for its existence and for the hard work and dedication you put into its creation.

In terms of the TCE approach, you must go a step beyond simply creating a book. To increase its market value, success is closely related to (a) how closely and clearly the working question matches the target market's need, (b) how you respond to that question, and (c) how well you inform that target market that you are asking that question, how fully you are answering it, and why it should care.

Sufficient material for a book?

Later you will gather material for your book. Here you are further defining the book's purpose and seeing how it will be unique. You also want to know if you'll be able to fill 100, 200, 300—you pick the length—pages of solid, valuable information.

Mostly this is done by seeing what others included in books similar to yours and determining whether you can do as well. Often the beginner is certain that there's no more than 30 pages of material anywhere in the world, while the veteran writer, looking at the same supply, wonders how he or she can possibly squeeze it into a salable length!

How long is long enough? As Abraham Lincoln said when asked how tall a man should be, "A man must be tall enough for his feet to touch the ground." The same for a book. It must be long enough to achieve its purpose.

Since one of the purposes of TCE books is to sell them profitably, most people have certain expectations related to page count (or at least book bulk) and what they will pay for it. So as a very rough guide, unless the contents are truly singular and worth a clearly perceived fortune (in which case any length will do), shoot for a minimum of about 100 pages, better 200. Beyond that it doesn't much matter.

Then your task is to estimate if you have information, or can get it, that will result in 125-200+ pages of copy, some of which is front and back matter, illustrations, chapter headings, and similar elements. If you don't come close, you have some choices: abandon the book, find what is missing, or sell the information by other means. This is a good time to guesstimate.

"Drive thy business or it will drive thee."

Benjamin Franklin (1706-90)

Chapter 7

MEETING THAT NEED THROUGH OTHER INFORMATION DISSEMINATION MEANS

If you accept the premise that "if you know something that others will pay to know, they will pay to know it many ways and by many means," you must now ask by which ways can you best share your information?

Up to this point I have assumed that an ink-on-paper book would be the most appropriate means of sharing, but it is time for you to test that assumption about your subject. And to identify, prioritize, and integrate the development of the other means while your book is being prepared, promoted, and published.

The path one follows here is nearly identical to that of Chapter Six. Except that first you must (1) identify the most appropriate means, then (2) see if somebody else is already, or soon will be, meeting those needs by those means, (3) develop a specific purpose statement, working question, and secondary questions for each means pursued, (4) see if there is sufficient material to create the sharing by that means, and (5) design a general working schedule for the creation and development of these means in relationship to the book.

Is a book the best way?
Is it time to re-evaluate?

While assuming that a book is the best way to share your information, I know that isn't always the case. (Still, for the purposes of this book, I will continue to make that assumption since for the vast majority of its readers it is so. For those for whom another means would be the best primary sharing tool, use the remainder of this text as a rough guideline for the other means and a more complete guideline for developing a book as a secondary tool.)

For all, now is the time to test the assumption before going any further.

When, for example, might a book not be the best primary sharing tool? The choreography of a ballet, while possible to explain on illustrated charts, would better be seen on a video. The score of a symphony comes in printed form; how it is performed by a certain orchestra would better be transmitted by a CD. The instant nationwide sharing of an opinion poll can't be done by book. Yet a book would be fine for a retrospective analysis or an explanation in depth.

What is clear is that most information is well shared by many means. What determines the primary means is the purpose of that particular sharing, time, and the economics of each means.

Comparing the information
dissemination means

One straightforward way of getting a global sense of the relationship between a book and other information dissemination means is to list them, then ask whether each means is appropriate (by a yes/no response and/or by assigning each a scaled, evaluative number, say 1-5, as to its relative appropriateness), and finally by comparing them by that appropriateness.

Other than a book, what means of information dissemination are most often used to share information the TCE way? In no particular order: articles, ebooks, audiobooks, newsletters, reports, talks, speeches, classes, seminars/workshops, audio cassettes or CDs, video cassettes, consulting, film, radio, TV, and, most recently, computer software. A comparison chart might look like this:

Means	Appropriate?	Rank of appropriateness
bound book		
digital book		
audio book		
articles		
newsletters		
reports		
talks		
speeches		
seminars/workshops		
classes		
audio CDs		
audio cassettes		
video		
consulting		
film		
radio		
TV		
computer software		

Another way to evaluate means, contents, markets, and more

Let me suggest a more playful approach to thinking about your book's subject and how it might be more widely shared, developed, and marketed. I call it topic-spoking, which I developed far more fully some years ago in ***Empire-Building by Writing and Speaking*** (see information in the "Other Sources and Guidelines" section near the end of this book). Here, let's simply introduce and explain the concept, then give an example.

First you draw a topic-spoking diagram, like the one that follows:

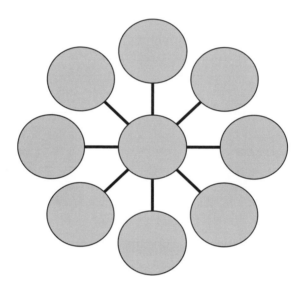

Then you write the word BOOK in the center of the diagram, as I've done on the diagram on the next page. Since you have a specific book in mind, you might then put the most appropriate information dissemination means by which more direct or related information could be shared at the end of each of the spokes. Use or add the spokes you need.

This is simply another way of doing what the comparison chart does, to select from many possibilities those means most likely to be useful and profitable for this particular subject. The chart can establish a ranking of appropriateness. That can be done on the topic-spoking diagram by putting the most appropriate in the top (or 12 o'clock position), the next most important next (at, say the 2 o'clock spot), and so on. The visual value of the diagram is that you can see each means in relationship to the others and begin, perhaps, to see ways that various means might be combined to provide even more or better ways of sharing and cross-promotion. A quick example would be combining articles or columns into an anthology (in book form) to be sold at speeches and talks.

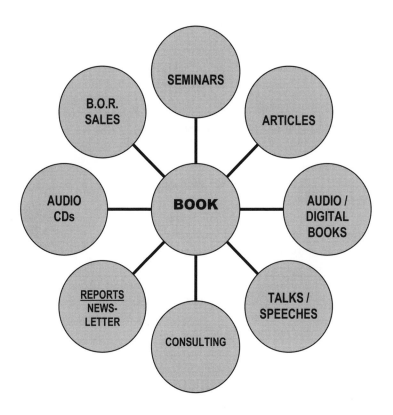

Then ask at each spoke how that topic might be shared by this means. What product or service could be developed to explain the topic that way? Which already exist? How might you build on them? How might that means be combined with another? Which new ways might you create?

The same format can be used many ways. Let's say that you want to sell this book to a related market. Instead of writing the book subject in the center, you might put that market instead, then see if the means also apply or see if there is a way to link the two markets, to stretch later sales.

Or you want to begin thinking about what this book might contain—its chapters or internal structure. You write in the center "Book Chapters" and at the end of the spokes you write down every chapter topic or title that comes to mind.

Topic-spoking can be used as many ways as you devise to stimulate your mind and create a fuller, more useful, and more profitable product.

Is somebody else already meeting the need by the appropriate means?

No guesswork here. If you've identified some means as appropriate ways to share your information beyond the book, before you invest much time or money you want to know who else is plowing those fields and how bountiful is their harvest. So speculation is replaced by some digging of your own.

You've already been to the library and know where to find books on the topic, plus you know the related headings. That familiarity should help you use the guides listed below. In addition, always ask the reference librarian for other, current research materials and see if different or new guides are available on the Web. "Google" is the new magic word.

ARTICLES: For magazine articles, check the library's computer equivalent to the older, printed *Reader's Guide to Periodical Literature* for articles in commercial publications, as well as equivalent indexes for articles in the various academic disciplines most closely related to your topic. For articles in newspapers, see newspaper indexes both from major cities, such as *The New York Times Index,* or those of newspapers nearest to or most interested in your topic.

NEWSLETTERS: Check *Newsletters in Print.*

REPORTS: Hard to locate. Find groups most likely to sell or release reports about the topic. Often they are trade or professional associations, so first find that group, then know what they publish. Check the annual *Encyclopedia of Associations* under "publications," which also includes reports, pamphlets, and cassettes, with the cost of each.

SPEECHES: It is very difficult to find out who is speaking about what. Major speeches are sometimes reported in the monthly magazine *Vital Speeches of the Day;* some of those and others appear in the annual book, *Representative American Speeches of* (current year). Another way is to check the topic category and listing titles of the speakers in the National Speakers Association at www.nsaspeaker.org.

SEMINARS: There is no central source, so you must check catalogs of seminars offered by colleges and universities, plus see what is offered to your specific market through professional or trade associations or to or through firms employing members of the potential market. Public seminars are often advertised through newspapers or by direct mail.

CLASSES: Get a current schedule of the institutions where classes about the subject might be taught.

AUDIO TAPES: For specific, current CD or DVD tapes available, check the monthly *Schwann Opus* as well as *The Penguin Guide to Compact Discs and DVDs*. For a complete guide to A-V reference periodicals and books, see *AV Market Place* (current year), published by Bowker.

VIDEO TAPES: The best here are *The Video Sourcebook* and **Bowker's** *Complete Video Directory.*

What do you do once you have the basic information? Follow the steps of Chapter Six, particularly (3)-(5) and the following (1)-(3), focusing each time on the information means in question. The idea is to see how much information is available about your subject by each means, how it is presented, how it is organized and packaged, how it is sold, its appearance and cost—in short, everything you need to know to do the same, where appropriate.

Do you really need a new purpose statement, working question, and secondary questions for each means?

The beauty of basic research is that information in one field or shared by one means can quickly be applied to another field or other means. An article telling how to cook quiche provides information that can easily be used in a book, in a video, or for a cooking class or seminar. So what you have already found out about your subject from books will serve as a solid base to share other ways. Why then would you need a new purpose statement and all that follows?

A different kind of sharing format brings with it a change in purpose and style, though often the differences are slight.

If the purpose statement of the article about cooking quiche is "to explain to readers, through words and two illustrations, the ingredients required and steps taken to prepare and cook quiche," then the purpose statement for a video with roughly the same intent would be different. It might be "to explain and show how to prepare and cook quiche, then to show, by using five different ingredients, how the viewer could convert the basic recipe into ten different quiches." The difference centers around "telling" in the article and "showing and telling" in the video.

With a different purpose statement comes a different working question and some different secondary questions. So you may need to develop these organizational tools for each means.

Is there sufficient material for each of the means you wish to pursue?

Again, like a book, here you can only estimate. But it's hard to imagine that if you have sufficient information to write a book you wouldn't have far more than you need to create most of the other means, such as writing an article, report, blog, podcast, radio script, or notes for a talk.

The one area where attention must particularly be paid concerns newsletters. Often they branch off and build from the book. That is, potential subscribers have read the book and now want more, new, vital information about the same or a very closely related subject. If possible, this can be a huge source of income and a vibrant core of an empire. But sometimes a subject is only one book deep. Trying to milk that book for newsletters would be useless once the cow was dry.

Designing an integrated schedule of other means around a book

The purpose of identifying the other means that you may pursue at this stage is to (1) reduce the preparation and marketing time for each of the means, (2) prevent any confusing overlap, and (3) increase your total income from all means.

What you are selling, remember, is expertise. As you establish that by one means, your displayed expertise also deserves attention in other ways. For example, who is a better candidate to speak about a subject than the person who wrote the book—or the reverse?

So here you take the most appropriate means from your earlier chart and see when they would best be developed as you write your book.

Let me share my own system, and biases, here. I like to talk with others about a topic as I research and put a book together. But I like to get paid to do that too. So as I formulate the premises of my book and gather examples, I create a seminar at the same time. Simultaneously, while I'm researching particular aspects of a topic, I gather additional information for very specific articles.

As you can see by my rather simple schemata on the next page, I start first by giving seminars through the extended education system. That allows me to put my concept into words, share it with paying listeners, and hear their questions and ideas, which in turn add to my knowledge and sharpen the contents of my book. At the same time I query about articles, following up positive responses with tailor-made pieces for those pages.

Somewhat later I write the book, and after it is published I sell it to many of those who attend the seminars (B.O.R sales) that I still offer, as well as to the earlier attendees, whose names I have.

From the book I produce an additional half-dozen or so articles. When these appear in print I include, in the biographical data with my name, information about the central website where all of these means are explained and sold, and how the book can be bought.

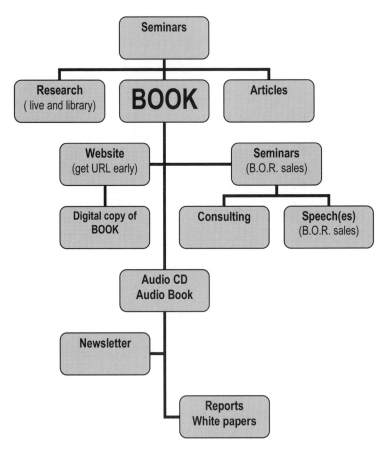

At some point fairly early on I develop an audio CD of the seminar, with the same in-class workbook, and this is made available to seminar participants, book buyers, and libraries. It also serves as a "demo" tape for groups or companies that want to book me as a speaker about that topic.

Speeches are generally sought about the time the book is published, as a result of the publishing promotion, the articles, the CD, or because a seminar participant wants me to share information with his/her organization or company. At some of those speeches, the book and/or CD series are made available after the presentation as back-of-the-room products. At others, they are bought in bulk when I'm booked and are given to every participant by the programmer or sponsor.

When the book appears, I also produce a digital version to see as a download, and might even produce an audio book. Somewhere along the way, as I become more knowledgeable about the topic, consulting begins, often the result of a person having read (or heard) my book or heard the seminar, the audio CD, the audio book, or a speech and wanting to apply the concept or adapt it to another problem. If reports or white papers are appropriate, they too are created.

Finally, while I don't produce newsletters (because they are simply too time-consuming), if I were to do so I'd begin after the book was out. My best market would be all of the clients who ordered the products or attended the seminar or a speech, plus those who had contacted me about the topic.

The early income from the seminars and articles helps pay initial expenses of research and book production, plus some of the promotion. And when the book is ready to be sold to my market, I also have the book as a download (less likely as an audio book), an audio CD, and a seminar to promote on the same flyer, plus a notation of my availability for speaking or consulting. Thus I'm selling one information core five or six ways, each costing me at most 20% of what it would cost to market separately. And I've helped scare off competition by planting myself firmly as an expert in each of the key fields before anyone can take the book concept and develop their products from it.

I nibble at the sides of my market with seminars and articles as I expand my information pool. Then I use my book as the primary full-market penetration tool. I sell the book hard the TCE way. And I wind up doubling income from all the other products and services that build on the same information and are mentioned in the same promotions.

That's really the "E" of TCE, for EXPANDED. If people will buy your information one way, they will almost always buy it many ways and by many means. I will expand upon this some in the third section of this book. But now is the time for you to do your groundwork and plant the seeds for profits by other means.

I've explained my thinking and the way I design a simple sketch to integrate other means into my book development. You must do this your way for your topic. Or not do it—at the very likely loss of considerable income at every facet of your subject's creation and development.

Chapter 8

DETERMINING WHERE AND HOW TO SELL YOUR BOOK TO THE NICHE MARKET

Once you have selected your market and have identified a particular market need to meet through your book, you must then determine where those in that market will buy your book. That, in turn, will help establish what the book must look like, what it should contain, and the tool you must develop to create sales.

Where do people usually buy books?

(1) at bookstores
(2) through the Internet
(3) at home or work, by mail
(4) at gatherings such as conventions or conferences
(5) at seminars, workshops, talks, or speeches
(6) at stores other than bookstores
(7) at public stalls or booths
(8) at garage or library sales
(9) at or through a school, generally for a class
(10) at or through a business
(11) at their door

To reach a sizable percentage of your targeted market, selling at some of the 11 locations will be ineffective. Bookstores (1), unless they are specific stores with a certain clientele seeking particular kinds of books, are far too general or imprecise to reach many of your niche market. Other stores, (6), suffer from that same imprecision. Both (7) and (8) are rarely found and deal in a small quantity of diverse products, and door-to-door selling (11), is atypical in the book market, even if the salesperson knew which doors belonged to your target market.

That leaves (2) the Internet, (3) by mail, (4) at gatherings such as conventions or conferences, (5) at seminars, workshops, talks, or speeches, (9) at or through a school, generally for a class, and (10) at or through a business.

Selling your book by mail

In most cases, selling your book by mail will probably be the most lucrative method, since TCE books are created for people who appear on accessible mailing lists and the potential buyers are, most likely, widely scattered and unaccustomed to finding or buying tightly-focused books at a bookstore.

Selling by mail means two things: (1) since the actual book won't be seen until after it is ordered, the book's cover needn't unduly attract attention; its appearance (presuming professional quality) won't much influence the sale, and (2) the promotional tool sent by mail to sell the book is extraordinarily important.

A second form of mail sales can also be quite profitable: other groups (usually publishers) with book clubs that they promote by mail. To participate you must get your book accepted by that club, often selling it to them at production cost plus 10% of the sale cost to their members. Let's say that you sell your book for $20 and it costs you $3.50 to produce. And that they will sell your book to their members for $15. You would receive the $3.50 plus 10% of the $15 sales cost, or a total of $5 for every copy sold to the book club, which would also pay for the shipping and for all promotion.

Since book clubs normally buy when the book is new, preferring to keep the production costs low by increasing the number of books run at the first printing, that can bring you quick, early cash. But it can also reduce your number of direct buyers if the book club is working your targeted market. The ideal situation is where you sell directly to your targeted market and the book club works a wider, related field you wouldn't mail to but that would also benefit from reading your book.

There is a third potential market using mail in its selling: mail order firms which will purchase the book from you, either in bulk or through drop-ship. The same care must be taken to preserve the core of the niche market for your own sales while using mail order groups to pick up secondary sales that you might otherwise miss. They usually expect a discount of 30-50% for each order processed, and will pay you for the drop-shipping. You also get the name and address of the buyer for your mailing list.

Selling your book through the Internet

However indifferent to or divorced from the Internet your buyership might be, digital sales can still add a bag of doubloons to your coffers. If your readers are techies or Web savvy, I'm preaching to the choir. Big bags.

First, you will have a website where your buyers will be directed. It will laud your book, provide the table of contents and a chapter or two to review, and tie the book to your other, related products. You aim them at your order page where excited browsers beg to buy.

To make that buy almost instant, you might adjust your book's contents some and create a .pdf digital version that they will order for a few bucks less (I guess to pay for the paper they might print it on). Others will buy the ink-on-paper version that you will mail to them.

You might also create an audio book that you will probably mail on discs.

You can also find other Internet folks or firms that work your side of the street selling similar information or services to your target market. You give them a discount to distribute your product directly or through your website (to capture the buyer's name). Or you create an affiliate program that rewards them for sending buyers your way.

At the same time you get on the promotion wavelength, using articles, blogs, podcasts, links or whatever is needed to let those digitally-driven know about your book and how it can be seen and evaluated at your website.

You get the book in all versions listed at Amazon.com and your digital version at the ebook outlets. And in all other sensible ways you tap into every outlet your most likely buyers would visit.

The problem is trying to strike some time/energy balance between the percentage of your buyers who will buy from the Internet and the others who will respond the other ways.

Selling your book at gatherings

Selling a TCE book at gatherings like conventions or conferences can work well if

(1) your targeted market has such gatherings,
(2) many (preferably most or all) of the members attend them,
(3) the attendance totals at each are fairly large,
(4) the number of such gatherings isn't excessive or they aren't too widely scattered,
(5) there is a means of selling books at the gatherings in a well publicized or much frequented area, and
(6) book purchases are encouraged.

This form of book selling would be even more effective if the participants were already aware of the book through an earlier mailing, from reviews, and if you spoke at the gathering and drew attention to the book's availability.

The drawback is obvious—the cost of the site, your living expenses and travel, and the lost production time spent working the gathering.

Selling your book at presentations

Seminars, workshops, talks, and speeches can be excellent ways both to make listeners aware of your book and to offer it immediately. What you say and how well you say it can have considerable impact on the book's sale. Buyers want more good things from an articulate, organized, informed source, and if your presentation shows you to be all of that, many sales should follow.

A request or permission to offer a seminar/workshop or a talk or speech usually comes because you have demonstrated your expertise through a book, which an organization often first hears about through a flyer you send in the mail. This then becomes a highly effective means of follow-up penetration; in turn, it sells more books and further validates your expertise.

The best news is that you usually get full price for every item sold—or you can bunch products and offer a 10-15% discount on the combo.

Selling your book for class or educational use

Teachers can be extremely effective in selling books. The very best kind of TCE book to sell this way would be one containing information necessary to receive a license or certification. If it were the only book with that information, it would be mandatory reading of every teacher, plus every student seeking that kind of validation.

Many books aren't that fortunate, but they can come close. Other than being the only book about the topic, a book can be the only one to approach the subject in a certain way. Or its strength can come from its clarity of explanation or its inclusion of new information not found elsewhere. Or the way it uses charts or illustrations or worksheets to convert the text to practical application. New laws, new requirements, new applications also breed new books.

Whatever unique quality your book has (and why would you publish a book if it weren't somehow unique?), that distinction must be brought to the teachers' attention. Free copies may have to be provided so teachers can review the text before adopting it. Which probably means mailing brochures first, plus some ground swell promotion through reviews, information in association publications, and so on.

Selling books for class or some educational use often produces a steady, growing long-term income base as new learners continue to enter the field.

Selling your book at or through businesses

Businesses can be quite influential in purchasing and promoting a TCE book. If the book meets a specific need of a business's employees, it will likely buy as many copies as it has employees who will benefit.

If the book helps a client or customer better understand, use, or desire a product or service offered by that business, it may well buy your book in large volume to sell or give to customers. Or it may negotiate with you to produce a modified version of your book to be used as a premium giveaway.

If your niche market works for just one or a few firms or most or all are affected by what a key firm does or says, that can have a huge influence on your book's sale and where it is bought. I.B.M. is an easy example of the latter. Whether friend, foe, or curious observer, computer folk cannot ignore I.B.M.'s action—or inaction. If your book uniquely addresses an I.B.M. product or service, and they buy it, that too cannot be ignored.

So if the needs of a business and the contents of your book overlap, your making your book's message and its availability known to that business can boost sales mightily. The degree to which this might affect the specific content of the book—the illustrations or in-house terminology used, for example—is directly related to the influence the business in question has on the targeted market or the quantity of books they will buy. If that's large enough, prepare an edition exclusively for that firm.

Your task now

First you must identify where your targeted market would buy your book, then list those locations in the order of buying likelihood. In the next chapter we will see what we must promise them to get them to make that purchase—and how we will make them aware of those promises.

Chapter 9

PROMISES THAT THE BOOK'S PROMOTIONAL TOOL MUST MAKE

Actually, more important than where your book will be bought is why. Why those in your niche market will reach into their pockets, pull out money, and buy a book knowing that they will still have to plow through hundreds of pages of prose before they reap an ounce of reward.

Your first foe is inertia. It's far easier to do nothing than something. Not to buy a book and not to read it, doing something else or nothing, all are inviting. So you must overwhelm inertia.

Your second foe is inaction. Inertia means remaining in a fixed condition without change. Inaction is the absence of action. They sound almost the same yet the difference, in terms of your profit, can mean poverty or wealth. Inactive buyers know that they should do something—like buy your book, read it, and reap the rewards—but they don't. They make a decision not to act.

One way to break the holds of inertia and inaction is to convince potential buyers that the rewards from buying your book and applying its contents can be so great, and so desirable, that only a fool would not do so.

You must make promises, or at least dangle lures, so bright and so convincing that the price and the effort to get and ingest the book are insignificant in comparison to what it will or could bring.

There's a catch: what you promise or dangle must be true! It is how you frame the truth and how you then get people to read it that we are discussing here—the promises the promotion must make and the kind of tool, and its contents, needed to get those promises before your potential buyers' eyes.

An antidote to inertia and inaction?

There is no universal cure to either lamentable condition. In TCE publishing, though, there's one remedy that almost always works: find a need desperately felt by your niche market, then show through your book how that need can be met.

The greater the desperation or the larger the number in your niche market who want to meet the need, the greater your book's selling potential. As important, you must highlight the benefits or rewards they can expect from meeting that need. And somewhere prominent in the promotional text they must be told in terms they can understand and apply that the book explains precisely what they need to know and do.

You have already identified your market's need. Now you must focus on what gets buyers to make the purchase: the benefits.

Identifying the benefits

Ask yourself, what rewards might your book buyer reasonably expect? Asking some additional questions might help:

(1) Why does the person have that need?
(2) When?
(3) Where?
(4) Who else has that need besides those in the target market?

Then list every reward, every positive and desired benefit that comes to mind for helping a person solve the need in each situation. Obvious benefits are love, joy, happiness, fulfillment. TCE benefits also include more income, greater prestige, a competitive edge, less toil, promotion, security.

Put the benefits one could expect from meeting that need in priority order as valued by your target market. Ask which benefits

Rewards =
- *More tips $*
- *Better @ job*
- *more confident*

would be sought the most by the greatest number of potential buyers. List every benefit from the most to the least likely.

Some benefits simply can't be provided by a book or by a book alone. They stretch beyond the reach of the written word and what it can do. But sometimes a book can tell all. So at this point you must determine which of those benefits, from the top of the list moving down, your book can bring its buyer, if applied as written. (If later research shows your list is too optimistic, you can delete the benefits that can't be met before you produce the final promotional tool.)

Said in a different way, what you tell the potential buyer creates a set of expectations. You say that the book can solve a problem or meet a need. That the buyer can expect certain rewards from that resolution. And that your book contains what they need to know. All of those promises, all of the expectations, dictate what your final promotional tool must include. Plus the necessary information about how the book can be ordered or bought, its cost, when it can be expected, what qualifies you to write it, and whatever else must be explained about its content to convince the buyer that it will do what you promise.

The promotional tool is your blueprint for action

The beauty of designing a promotional tool as you are creating a book is the single-mindedness of its intent and the focus it provides for research and writing.

Earlier you wrote a purpose statement, converted it into a working question, and from that produced a general ideological framework for your book. Secondary questions gave it a rough outline. Now you are asking why those in your targeted market would want to buy this information. What benefits would they receive? From this you are creating a rough promotional tool.

Later you will conduct the actual research and write the book. Your rough outline will take final form, probably with alterations and some redirection. Some of the original promises proposed to the buyer may be less clear; new promises may emerge. So you may have to adjust the final promotional tool.

Why you develop an initial promotional tool now is to provide guidance to help determine the particular avenues of inquiry you must pursue to make the book valuable and marketable. By tentatively identifying the selling promises now, you are also narrowing the range of necessary information you must gather at the research and writing stage.

The promotional tool gives you a standard against which you can ask: does that information fulfill the book's promises?

Which does not mean that the truth is in any way compromised or that the only facts that are admitted are those which support the book's predetermined theme. It means that the book is written for a very specific purpose to an identified target market and that everything included meets the rigorous scrutiny of acceptable research. But it has one function only, to meet a specific need. And through how the book meets that need, promises can be made to those who apply its contents, promises that will be modified in the final promotional tool as necessary.

A quick review of where we are and how we got here

Sometimes it is refreshing and enlightening to put what we've shared into a capsulated perspective, to show in a slightly different way what this chapter is about. Three steps of a quick review:

(1) Much of the success of the TCE approach comes from the clarity with which you identify (a) your target market, (b) the needs it will pay to meet by book and other information dissemination means, and (c) the ways by which you make that market aware of those needs and your ability to meet them.

(2) Your promotional tool(s) must (a) tell potential buyers of your book that they have a need and what it is, (b) how they would benefit from meeting that need, (c) how your book will help them do that, and (d) why they should buy your book now.

(3) To do that you (a) must identify the specific target market most likely to buy your book, (b) customize that book's content to meet at least one key need of that specific target market, (c) provide actual and obvious help to meet that need in your book, and

(d) let all potential buyers of your book know that the book that can help meet their need is available, why it should be bought, and where and how it can be obtained.

How can you tell potential buyers to buy your book?

There may be 100 different ways, but most niche buyers become aware of books by:

(1) a flyer or brochure in the mail
(2) copy, links, ads, or website display on the Internet
(3) a space or classified ad in a magazine, journal, newspaper, newsletter, etc.
(4) a display in a bookstore, at a convention or seminar, etc.
(5) a review in a publication
(6) a review on radio or TV
(7) referral in an article or book—any form of print media
(8) referral on radio or TV—any form of other media
(9) referral by the author in a speech, seminar, etc.
(10) personal referral from another person
(11) use as a textbook or as required or suggested reading
(12) an actual copy in a library, bookstore, or other location
(13) a news release about the book or author
(14) an award for the book or author
(15) a book list
(16) a book club
(17) a card deck received in the mail
(18) a catalog
(19) telephone solicitation

In the previous chapter it was determined that TCE books would most likely be sold six key ways: by mail, on the Web, at gatherings, at oral presentations, for a class, or at or through a business. The book would either be sold by a flyer or on display, though the latter would be enhanced by informing the niche market by mail of the book's existence and purpose. Therefore, our focus here is on a mailer: a flyer or brochure.

What must your flyer do?

Why are you promoting your book? Because you want to sell it to at least 10% of your targeted market, which by conventional direct mail standards is exceptionally high. Therefore, to reach this goal your flyer must convince its recipient that

(1) he or she has a pressing need or problem,

(2) your book offers an (immediately) applicable solution,

(3) it is either the only way that solution can be obtained or it is the best solution available,

(4) meeting the need or solving the problem is far more valuable than the cost of the book,

(5) your credentials or expertise give you the authority to offer this solution,

(6) the solution is fully and professionally explained, and

(7) your book should be bought now!

Even more, the flyer must do these four things:

(1) reach the decision maker's hands;

(2) inform, convince, sell;

(3) make the ordering process quick and simple, and

(4) look as good or better than the book itself.

To do those things, what must it contain? A detailed study of other, excellent book-selling fliers is in order, particularly those sent to your target market. What is the competition? What are they circulating? What must you include? What can you do better?

I can only give a general reply here, based on a review of a wide variety of such fliers. Most include the following:

(1) a headline featuring a benefit or need

(2) the book's title prominently displayed

(3) copy telling why the book should be bought

(4) the book's cost

(5) how the book is bound

(6) testimonials about the book and/or author

(7) references (sometimes testimonials too) about earlier, related books by the author

(8) excerpts from the book

(9) an illustration or photo of the book (cover[s])

(10) a photo of the author

(11) biographical information about the author emphasizing qualifications related to the book being promoted

(12) a table of contents

(13) an order form with an address, credit card fill-in instructions, to whom a check should be written, shipping costs, tax information, lines for the buyer's address and ZIP, and sometimes a number for credit card orders by phone or fax

(14) sometimes a return envelope, sometimes with prepaid postage

How much of the flyer must you prepare now?

You must know the promises you will make and the expectations you will create to get your book bought. They should be written out at this stage, word-by-word, precisely and clearly. (You can modify them later.)

That is no simple task. It provides the spine and direction of your research and writing. It is very important. You must know while you research, write, and produce the book what its buyers will expect to see on its pages, the hooks you must emphasize to induce them to buy. Also, the particular benefits they can expect from their purchase, the guidelines and how-to information and processes, and so on, that you have promised to include in your book to help them meet a need.

That's it. No preliminary drawings, no ad copy or typesetting. Later, when the artwork for the book's cover exists, when you know how long the book will be, when you know how many of the original promises can be made and kept, when you have a good photo of yourself, and when 100 more details can be answered, then it is time for the selling tool(s) to be sculpted. Identify the heart now. Build the body later.

"Genius hath electric power
which earth cannot tame."

Lydia M. Child (1802-80)

Chapter 10

IS THE BOOK WORTH PUBLISHING?

To this point you have been forming a book from the rough clay of ideas and hope, to mold it into some early, recognizable form. Yet books are major investments to create and publish. They cost in time, energy, and plain old cash.

Energy is a given at each step. I have tried to reduce the time investment at the planning stages to the minimum, aware that every idea doesn't result in a book. In fact, most drop out by now, so keeping the time investment small gives you more time to pursue other, stronger ideas or other, non-book ventures.

Here the third element, cash, becomes a factor, before you fire that clay into its final form. The questions are simple: how much will it cost? Do you have, or can you get, enough capital to finance the book? And will the profit earned be worth the time, energy, and money spent?

We need some starting numbers to make evaluative decisions. So let's revert to an earlier goal—the $50,000 profit from the book explained in Chapter 2—and move backward from there, plugging in, for the sake of calculation, 2007 cost figures supported by 30+ years as a publisher. (I know, $50,000 profit seems like peanuts in the 21st century—unless you don't have it. But if you can earn $50,000 rather quickly from the book, usually there's at least another $50,000 from ancillary products, consulting, speaking, or teaching not far behind that comes from the book's existence. Also, the root of what can be a seven-figure empire is planted, waiting for a clever, industrious, slightly daring soul to make it happen.)

The cost of earning a quick
$50,000 profit from your book

A standard publisher would have to sell 19,165 books at $20 @ to pay you $50,000 in royalties at today's conventional royalty rates. How many books would you need to write, self-publish, and sell to reap the same income—in a quarter of the time?

Again, some basic facts: you want $50,000 profit from a $20 book. Say it costs you 50% of that $20 to produce and promote your book and that by using the TCE approach you intend to sell to 10% of your targeted market. Thus $20 divided by 2 = $ 10 profit per book.

Let's see how much it will cost you to earn $50,000.

Initial book production costs: $11,500

You would need the initial book production costs first:

Research	$ 1,000
Overhead	500
Cover preparation	1,000
Illustrations	1,000
Printing (5000 books)	7,050
Shipping	<u>950</u>
	$ 11,500

Some of the numbers require a brief explanation. First, I have no idea if you need to spend any money for research. You might already know everything anyone would want to read about your subject, in which case this money stays in your pocket. The same with overhead: you may be using the company computer during lunch time and hand delivering the mail. So adjust these numbers accordingly. You'll likely need some funds for both, though.

It is no facile cliché that a book is judged (and bought) by its cover. So you spend to have a cover professionally designed and prepared for the printer. Yet in the TCE mode you will sell mostly by mail and the book will more likely be bought because it meets a dire need. Thus your cover needn't be as flashy; on the other hand, it must photograph clearly and look sharp. The demands are different but the cost won't be far less. $1,000 should easily cover the cover.

Illustrations are the great unknown. If you use charts or other computer-aided graphics, $1,000 will be far too much since you will likely create them yourself. If you use intricate artwork drawn by a professional, it may not be enough. Adjust accordingly.

Printing the book may run you about 10% of its ultimate cost—more if the illustrations need to be in colors other than black and white. And much more if you produce very small quantities. (It will cost at least twice as much per book to print 500 copies as it will 5,000.) I'm presuming about 200 pages, all b/w but the cover, a trade paperback. For 5,000 copies it may cost $7,050, at about $1.40 each.

Shipping is also an unknown. Too often your best bids are printed somewhere across the country, which means you must pay to get the books to your warehouse. $950 is my calculation, again to be adjusted to your reality.

Promotional costs: $23,250

Next you will need promotional funds. The artwork must come first, of course. The rest will be spent to buy niche direct mail addresses and prepare and mail fliers to them:

Flyer art preparation	$ 1,500
Mailing list: $ .06 @	3,000
Print/mail at $ .375 for 50,000	18,750
	$ 23,250

The flyer you will send to your targeted market is the single most important selling tool you will create. So put its creation in the hands of professionals who turn out quality products, probably with a good graphic artist or an ad agency. Shop around and make certain that the flyer says what it must to appeal to your buyers. $1,500 is probably too much.

A well conceived flyer is no better than its appearance in final, printed form. Make certain that your printer produces a mailer worth that initial investment and the huge postage costs that follow. That is, bid printers carefully, see what they have produced, and get your costs and deadlines clear and firm. Then contact a mailing house to send the fliers to your mailing list by bulk rate. You should be able to mail a classy item to your market for about $18,750. The postage part of that ($11,650) must be paid before anything is sent so you can calculate the number of items you can afford to mail with available cash at, in this case, $ .233 per item mailed, using the mailing house bulk permit.

Fulfillment and tax reserve funds: $5,775

State tax and shipping/postage should be paid by the buyer, although a contingency fund must be set aside for those who don't include the money in their order. (It's easier to pay it than try to get it from these losers, frankly.)

Then when they order you must package and ship the book their way. That's called fulfillment, and whether you do this yourself or you farm it out to someone else, figure it will cost you about $1 an order, which we will calculate high here at $1 a book. The tax reserve is arbitrarily calculated at the current California rate of 7.75% (of $20) for approximately 500 books.

Tax reserve fund	$ 775
Fulfillment	5,000
	$ 5,775

Do you have, or can you get, enough capital to finance the book?

Using the figures above, it will cost about $40,525 to earn $50,000 profit. That means you must gross $90,525 to keep the $50,000. Or a 123% return.

It's actually better than that. The $40,525 is puffy. You should pay less for the book production, the tax reserve fund is a bit fictitious (you may never need much of it), and fulfillment should cost less. Let's realistically think $40,000 for costs.

Still, hardly anybody has an extra $40,000 sitting around waiting for a book to be written, produced, and sold. No bank will ante up that kind of money for an amateur with a book in mind, without a big house or a fleet of new cars to back it up. Even investment brokers aren't that balmy.

You'll have to have the money yourself, get it from a relative or literary angel (with an 800 number in heaven), go into hock, or find some other source. Sobering possibilities.

But don't despair. You can get by for about $10,000. It's just much, much faster—and the return is that much quicker—the more you can invest at the outset.

You see, you don't need all $40,000 on the first day. You can invest the profits you make as the book sells to generate money to cover later expenses. Let's follow three scenarios, leaving you to imagine a hundred deviations.

When do you need money— and how much?

The fat cat approach: a low-risk "bet the farm"

This presumes you have the initial $11,500 for book production, you provide the text digitally, have a fine looking cover produced, and print 5,000 copies of the book .

You can afford the flyer art preparation, its printing, and the full mailing to all 50,000 lucky recipients. Another $23,250—a total of $34,750.

The rest you can pull from profits. The tax/postage fund and the fulfillment costs can be paid from the $90,525 you are going to get when the books sell since they occur only at the time of purchase. In short, even financial fat cat daredevils only initially need $34,750 to make a $50,000 profit. Best yet, since they print the books and mail all of the fliers at the same time, half of the money can be expected in 30 days and 98% in 13 weeks, if the direct mail industry is right. (Add a few more weeks on both ends.)

The skinny cat approach: you sleep better with less at risk

If you've got $20,000, the first $11,500 is going to cover the initial book production costs. You will print all 5,000 copies of the book, probably storing them in your garage or basement.

You know that you will earn that last fulfillment/tax reserve of $5,775 as the books are sold, so that leaves $8,500 to invest in promotion. The first $1,500 goes to flyer art prep. The remaining $7,000 must pay for part of a mailing list plus flyer printing and mailing, which means you can print and mail exactly 16,092 fliers—let's say 16,000. At a 10% sale ratio, you can expect to earn $32,000, minus the $1,600 for fulfillment; let's say $30,000, setting $400 aside for the tax/postage fund.

But you still have 34,000 fliers to send. The mailing list and mailing will require $14,790 of the $30,000. When you sell your 10%, you will bring in another $68,000, from which you set aside $3,400 more for fulfillment and $375 for the tax, leaving $64,225.

So in this scenario it takes several months longer to mail two waves of fliers but you risk about $15,000 less. You sleep better in those first weeks.

I would do it a bit differently, however. Rather than having just 16,000 fliers printed, I would arrange to have all 50,000 done, paying half in advance and half in 30 days (or all in 30 days), mailing to all I can from what remains of my $7,000 (about $4,600). Within 30 days I will have earned from books sold far more than my debt to the printer, and as the books continue to sell, I would continue to have my already printed fliers mailed out, until the market is covered. That way I get the fliers done cheaper in bulk and I have them ready to mail the day my postage money is in hand.

The drawback for the skinny cat? Time. The quicker the fliers are out, the faster the profits return. So sending fliers out in two or several spurts simply delays the money coming back.

Another modest disadvantage? The timing. If you plan to follow up or coordinate the book's release with other selling means, or a publicity campaign, it is hard to do so effectively with the items creeping into the market in successive mailings.

The alley cat approach: less money up front, more hustle, smaller profits

You start with $10,000. With that you pay the initial book production costs, except that you will print only 1,500 copies of the book. That will reduce the book cost (at $2.30 each) to $3,450 (and the shipping to $300), leaving you with an operating kitty of $2,750.

You're also going to pick apart those initial book production costs. You will write a book with little or no research costs or you will absorb them into your other living or job expenses. The same with overhead. And you'll try to design the book without costly illustrations.

Where you can't afford to scrimp is in the contents, appearance, and cover. The book must be stylistically at the level of other books your market buys, and the cover must be good and professional looking. I'm always assuming the content is exceptional.

Add to your $2,750 a potential income of $30,000 from the sale of the 1,500 books. So here you have choices. You can set aside direct mail and go for direct sales, using the kitty to get a display booth at the convention or workshops or speeches where your target market gathers. At the same time you focus on the low-cost promotions we mentioned in Chapter 8 that draw orders and eyes to your website. Get the book widely reviewed, send comp copies to the most important decision makers in the field, request testimonials, and directly contact all you know to get those 1,500 copies bringing in money to finance your direct mail.

Then buy a mailing list, have fliers printed, and, as you can afford it, send out the fliers. After the 1,500 copies are gone, print again in quantities the continual direct mail sales can support.

Eventually, you will mail to 50,000, but it may take six months or a year. And your profits will be less because you must buy the mailing list and book printing in smaller (more expensive) quantities, and you must pay the artwork, fulfillment, and tax reserve on the run or as needed.

Another drawback to this approach is the loss of the timing impact that comes from mailing the fliers all at once, with the promotional, publicity, and follow-up advantages that could bring.

Whatever scenario you use or invent, we should look at other ways you can gather more selling income.

The website

We have mentioned before that you need a website as a central station and selling house for your empire—or for just one book. The process is easy enough. Find a URL that buyers quickly identify with your core topic or your book title. If your book is about empire building, and that title is taken, reserve www.building-your-empire.com. You get the idea. Work with a reliable server, create an easy-to-navigate website with the minimum of gaudy distractions, direct the seeker to your book, your purpose, you, and all of your products—plus the all-important ORDER FORM, on an easier-to-understand page, preferably with a shopping cart buying process as soon as orders justify its cost.

Once they find the book page, it should sell the book's benefits, how those are attainable by the reader, the book's contents, others' praising testimonials, a biography of the writer, the book's front and back cover, and one or several free sample chapters, preferably the first and a meaty one later on.

Also delicately woven into the book copy are benefit-laden references plus links to other products you have produced and they can also buy at the linked ORDER FORM. In fact, all of your services—speaking, consulting, project direction—should also be evident, and each product and service should have its own linked page, plus its content explanation, testimonials, covers, and some more free samples.

This is also where you can create and sell ebooks, courses, and all-product bundles, with their rather labyrinthine carrot-and-stick opening pages that have, or should have, the reader salivating for the product by the time they have read eight or ten pull pages. Alas, this is not the book that explains that approach or process, but it must be seriously considered as one of several business models when you design your empire and its integrative website.

Other promising paths

Six other paths were promising for TCE books: to book clubs, to other mail order firms dealing in similar books, at gatherings (probably conventions or conferences), at presentations (seminars, workshops, talks, and speeches), for class use, and to or through a business.

In Chapter 9 we mentioned 18 more ways that you can tell potential customers about your book.

Don't overlook the most obvious: talk directly to the 15 or 20 people you know best in that market and sell them. Move out from there. Talk to your local association chapter, then the state, then the national convention. Set up a booth. Comb the market to get others to sell your books, giving them the standard 20-40% discount if bought in lots of 10 or more. Talk to teachers who would benefit from using your book as a text. Talk directly to businesses; sell by phone. Do the things you would do after the direct mail solicitation if you were a fat, or even skinny, cat. Do it in reverse. Alley cats persevere.

Will the profit earned be worth the time, energy, and money spent?

Only you can answer that. We are calculating a 50% profit. For every dollar you put up, you get it plus another dollar back—quickly. We actually saw a 123% return in this book's rather typical example. Financially that should satisfy anyone.

As for energy, that's what gets the money doubled. You run the risk and put in the effort rather than letting another publisher do both and give you royalties of 15% or less. Is it worth your effort?

And time. If you write a book rather than earn a million dollars another way, and earnings are your criterion, then it isn't worth it. But if you write a book after hours or in your spare time and the book and writing means much more to you than the dollars alone, any profit is a boon.

To determine whether the profit is worth the time, calculate the hours it will take you to prepare, produce, and publish the book. Convert that into a dollar rate, so much per hour. Add that to the costs of the book. Subtract that from the gross income (or anticipated gross income) and what remains is profit. Then answer the question yourself: is it worth it?

Chapter 11

PICKING A TITLE, CREATING TESTING TOOLS, AND TESTING THE BOOK

Nothing sells a book quicker than its title, particularly by mail. In one glance the title must explain what the book is about and why a person would want to buy it.

The title is the headline that gets its readers to want to read more. The hook that brings them in. It seizes their attention in a second to buy hours and hours of profitable reading. Or gets your book ignored.

So here is where you write down 10 to 25 or more possible titles as they come to mind. Only later, after the contents are fleshed out and you see what you're actually sharing with readers, will you select your final title.

Some title restraints

There are things to consider when selecting a title, though none is as important as this:

"Without using deception, the title must sell the book."

Some titles do that better than others. They are usually short, catchy, accurate, and appropriate.

Short means just what it says: few words. Six or less are the easiest to remember. More than six usually requires the title to be run as a double-decker or, horrors, a triple-decker: lines atop each other on the flyer and cover. The problem is reader resistance if the title is long and dense. Yet many a good title has been long. Few are dense.

"Catchy" is just that. It catches your eye or ear. It twists a cliché or plays on a common phrase. A word or sound piques your interest. Still, many a good title isn't catchy. *Gone With the Wind* is; *The Holy Bible* isn't.

Accurate gets to integrity. You don't want to sell a book through a title that misleads buyers into thinking the text is about something altogether different. And appropriate refers to tone. A formal academic book shouldn't be titled in vulgar slang. The language tone and theme of the book should be expressed in the words used in the title. *The Compleat (sic) Practical Joker* and *Gray's Anatomy* are appropriately titled.

You might consider using some of the 14 words said to be the most persuasive in the English language, if accurate and appropriate to your book: new, how to, save, discover, safety, health, free, you, guarantee, love, easy, money, proven, and results. These words demonstrate another point made by Winston Churchill that, when given choices, seek old words rather than new, short words rather than long. Comfortable words known to the reader. Use polysyllabic jawbreakers at peril, unless that is what your book is about!

Finally, you cannot copyright a title, though in certain (rare) instances part or all of a title can be protected as a trademark. Others' titles are usable by you, as your title can be purloined by them. Best to plow new ground, though, to avoid any confusion that another's title might create.

Why do you need a title now, even if you might, on the long shot, change it later to bring it closer to the book's contents? Because you want to test the book before you invest any more time or money and you can't test a book without some title!

Two kinds of test marketing

You want to write and produce a book that will sell to a maximum number of people for minimal promotional cost. You also want to do that in the best, quickest, and most profitable way. Therefore you need two tests:

(1) To see what form of publishing is best for you.
(2) To see what percentage of your target market will buy your book at what cost.

Which form of publishing best meets your needs?

We must reconsider both forms of publishing again at this step. To reiterate, in standard commercial publishing a firm accepts a manuscript, produces and prints it as a book, sells it, and pays the writer a small percentage of what it earns from each book sold.

By the other process the writer writes a book (or finds a written book), produces it, has it printed, receives the bound volumes, and sells them. Called self-publishing, the writer's profits come after expenses have been paid.

Sometimes there is a mix. A standard publisher may buy a writer's self-published books in final, printed form and distribute them. A writer may decide to reprint a book that was earlier produced and sold by a standard publisher and went out of print. Or the writer may contract with a standard publisher to buy back a certain number of books to sell to his or her own market. At this step, let's focus on the unmixed examples of commercial versus self-publishing, plus the last type of mix.

Sometimes there is no choice at all. Standard publishers aren't interested in the writer's book. Or they might be interested if the contents were slanted differently or written to a different readership, but the writer is adamant that the book will be done one way for one particular readership—so it's self-publishing or no publishing at all.

Therefore, to determine which form of publishing is best, you must first see if any standard publisher is interested, then calculate the likely income from each. Or you may simply decide that self-publishing is it. Now is when the steps to make that choice are made.

How to test standard publishers

First, why would you test them at all?

Because if you can get other publishers to do the editing, printing, promotion, and marketing and still receive what you wish for your writing labors, you will save enough time to write another book—or do anything else equally as exciting—while they tend to the publishing chores!

Secondarily, if they are willing to invest their money and pay you big returns, they predict sufficiently large sales to pay themselves a far greater return. Which may tell you that self-publishing would be even more profitable for you. (I have a friend who will not self-publish a book that a standard publisher doesn't want; he relies on their gut reaction and testing, as it is, to tell him if he has a winner!)

What do publishers want to know? The current *Writer's Market* is the best guide. It lists about 100 pages of publishers, each telling in detail what they publish and how (or if) they want to be approached.

For the most part you will use one of two approaches, (1) a book proposal for many bids, and (2) a query letter with attachments for one-at-a-time solicitations.

While bidding by proposal (sending simultaneous queries and a sample chapter to many publishers) covers far more ground much quicker, it is so seldom successful for newcomers that I will simply suggest the most recent editions of two books for you to follow should you wish to pursue that route: Michael Larsen's *How to Write a Book Proposal*, published by Writer's Digest

Books, and *Write the Perfect Book Proposal,* by Jeff and Deborah Levine Herman, with excellent proposals one can use to create their own.[1]

The most successful route is, alas, the slowest. But it shows you to best advantage and allows you to market your idea before and while you write the actual book. It requires you to select a topic, then answer five basic questions:

(1) Who would read your book?
(2) Why would they buy it?
(3) Where would they use it?
(4) What else is available?
(5) How does your book differ?

Particularly important is that you know which publishers are working your target market, as well as those books similar to yours in the current *Subject Index to Books in Print* and *Forthcoming Books.* Those will be the publishers you want to approach first.

Review your working question. Your book will be the answer to it. Around that theme and the replies to the five basic questions above, write a two-page query letter to the publisher you would most like to handle your book. Subsequently, query other publishers that work your market, one at a time, in decreasing preference.

Since you have already studied your market closely and have an idea of how to sell to it, include that information in your query—or on an attached page. Be specific with numbers and facts: the size of your target market, other markets with similar interests, the need your book meets, what other books exist that address that need, and how yours does it better (and why). Don't include your promotional tool or ideas you have about non-book means by which you can also sell that information.

---

[1] See "Other Sources and Guides" starting on page 189.

With the query send (1) an outline of your book's contents or an annotated table of contents, (2) a one-page synopsis, if necessary, and (3) a reference/resource sheet that explains the major printed sources you will draw from for your book's contents, in annotated bibliographical fashion, and the people you will interview, in annotated biographical form.

Do you mention that you want to receive $50,000 profit from the royalties (and double that on your own later by non-book means)? Not the doubling, and perhaps not the $50,000 either. You want them to reply affirmatively first; then you can talk money.

Using our $20 book and the 10-12.5-15% of list royalties as a base, the standard publisher would have to sell 19,165 copies for you to realize your $50,000. Will your niche market yield that kind of a sale? Will the publisher sell directly to that market, preferably by mail? And if the publisher does sell by mail, will you receive a lower royalty?

If your query and attachments get you to the money-talking stage, you need to know those things, plus:

(1) What is your advance against royalties? When is it paid?
(2) When do you receive royalties? Quarterly? Less often?
(3) How much is withheld each time for returns and damages?
(4) When will the book appear?
(5) What happens if between approval of the final, corrected manuscript and its publication the publisher aborts the book?
(6) What unchangeable (and unacceptable) stipulations exist in the contract about rights to future books or the use of the information of the book in question?
(7) How much of the budget will be pegged for promotion to the target market? When and how will it be used?
(8) What track record does this firm have with other writers of similar books? (The last point can be easily checked: contact the writers directly and ask.)

In the meantime, the publisher, upon receiving your package, will judge your idea, marketing figures, and writing skills. If impressed, you will likely be asked to send several (usually three) sample chapters. If still interested, a contract is generally drawn. Your advance (against royalties) is paid in part when the contract is signed, in part when the final corrected manuscript is submitted, and (at times) when the book is actually published.

Package your idea to highlight its value, need, and marketability and sometimes you will find one (or many) publishers eager to run the risk, do the selling, and keep 85-90% of the gross income.

Those are the realities.

Let me insert here one of several ways that double-win thinking and clear contracting might help offset the huge financial sacrifice one makes when others publish their book(s).

A double win: buying back books from another publisher

Sometimes a "deal" can be made with another publisher, so you can sell your book at a higher profit to a selected market.

Let's say that you offer seminars and those who attend are unlikely to be influenced by the publisher's promotional campaign. You may want to buy a set number of books to sell directly to that group.

The conventional, and far less profitable, way is simply to buy them as needed from the publisher. The standard discount starts at 40% for ten or more; very rarely, it can go up to 50% for large quantities. Often a publisher will not pay you your royalty on those purchases, so one concession you might seek in your contract is to receive both the conventional wholesaler's discount and your royalty.

A better "deal" follows the system often used by book clubs. As a book is being printed, book clubs buy an additional number of books from that same printing, thus lowering the publisher's per-book printing cost while reducing their own cost. They then pay the publisher 10% of the cost of the book to their own club member and agree to limit sales exclusively to that group. They receive a better than 80% discount.

So why not follow a similar model, sort of in reverse, that will get you a hefty discount? If you know that you can sell a handsome number of books within a year or two (say 3,000) to your seminar participants, why not ask the publisher to add on 3,000 books to the print that you will buy at 20% of the retail cost, payable in part by your advance against royalties, and by cash for the remainder, all with the understanding that you will not compete with their selling venues. Of course, you won't receive royalties for the books you sell and the publisher will probably ask you to agree in writing to limit the sales specifically to the markets you suggest (and thus not openly compete)—very acceptable conditions for such a profit ratio.

How would that work with our example and still earn you $50,000? Let's say that you want to order 3,000 copies of the book to sell at $20, the list price. To simplify the calculations, let's say:

(1) you are paying $4 a book for 3,000 books that you will sell for $20; that is the cost of printing, prep, and the 20% charge they assessed;

(2) you will not receive your advance of $5,000; rather you will pay the publisher $7,000 additional cash, and

(3) you will pay $500 for shipping.

Your potential income from 3,000 books at $20 each is $60,000, minus the $7,000 you paid up front to the publisher and the $500 for shipping. So regardless of the selling prowess of the publisher, you are already $2,500 ahead of your $50,000 goal—assuming you sell all 3,000. Since we have seen that most of your royalties are received in the second year of the publisher's sales, and you are expecting to sell these back-of-the-room books in two years, this is a wise step for you and beneficial to the publisher as well since they received the first printing at a rock-bottom price, they had to pay no advance against royalties, you assumed a sizable portion of the initial risk, and the presence of groundswell selling on your part should create interest and demand for bookstore, book club, and library purchases, which is their domain.

So you will start selling once the books arrive, pay off that $7,000 debt with the first 350 books sold, and be earning good income the first year (about $30,000 minus the $7,000). You will continue to earn that amount the second year.

The best news is that, without an advance, you will also earn royalties from the first day of the publisher's sales, which will increase your ante considerably.

When do you replenish your stock of 3,000 books? Either when the publisher goes back to print (just strike up a new deal) or, if the publisher decides not to return to print, when the rights are ceded to you. Which means you must pay particular attention to that facet of your contract so that the book becomes yours quickly after it is abandoned by the publisher. (Then you just self-publish it, meeting your market needs as well as those previously met by the publisher.) When the book becomes yours is the ideal time to update and release a second edition!

Testing your book in your target market

The best way to see if anybody in your target market will buy your book is to ask them. Simple.

But not so simple.

If you know people in the target market, can you trust their responses—or will they just say "yes" because you are a friend? If you don't know them, how do you know that they are representative of the larger market? Is there a danger that somebody you tell will beat you to the market with their issue of a similar book? And how can you find out how much people will really pay? Given choices, won't everybody pick the lowest price?

To select people to be tested, keep the number fairly small and limit yourself to the target market. You already know how they can be found by mailing list, but generally the minimum number of names the list renter will provide is several thousand or the minimum cost is $100+.

Nonetheless, you might contact the mailing list manager and explain what you are doing: you will rent their full list later but you'd like to test a sample (say 50-200) now, and could you get those names on pressure-sensitive labels for a low, introductory price, like free? Sometimes they will agree!

If not, you must pick (a) friends, (b) others in the target market suggested by friends, (c) target market members chosen in other ways, or (d), pay the minimum list rental cost.

Friends, as suggested earlier, aren't too reliable. They would rather tell you what they think you want to hear than what they really feel. And who has 50-200 friends from a target market? Still, there are friends who will understand why objectivity is so important and they would be asked.

Friends' friends are often a better source, particularly if the person recommending them doesn't talk about the book first.

Perhaps the best way is to use a list of members in the target market (such as an association membership list, names from club rosters, professional listings in the phone book, etc.). If your book is to be national in scope, this also allows you to test in various areas of the United States. There is no way to be certain that what this test group says represents all of the other members of the target market, of course. But the larger your test group, the more likely it will be fairly representative.

How do you protect your book's idea? In truth, there is no way to protect an idea other than to keep it to yourself. So you must take a risk if you want to see if others will buy your book, since to respond they must know what the book is about.

Avoid including specific people in the group tested: association officers or others with widespread market contacts, media folk, seminar-givers or book writers in the field, or anybody else you suspect might put your idea or information in print.

And keep the number tested small and select, make your presentation to them professional in tone and appearance, imply that the book is nearly ready for release, and tell them only what is necessary for them to make a valid response.

What will you send them? First determine what you want to know. Probably whether they would be interested in buying a book at some future date about your subject at a stated price.

Draw from your promotional tool, your title, and whatever else you know or imagine about your book and prepare an information sheet that describes your book's purpose, contents, length (pick an approximate page length that is divisible by four, better by 16), cost, type of binding (probably cloth or paperback), and illustrations. You needn't know the design details—style, type font, and so on—to sell the book nor must it contain an example of the final cover or your photo. Simply enough information, particularly about the contents and benefits, to give the recipient a solid grasp of what you will produce.

(See examples in the Case Study at the end of this book.)

Then compose a letter to accompany the information sheet in which you ask its recipient for a favor, a quick 30-second reply to the questions in the enclosed questionnaire. The questionnaire can be a postcard or a 3" x *5"* index card with a self-addressed envelope. Explain in the letter that you are in the final stages of completing work on the book described in the enclosed information sheet and simply need a sense of the target market's response so the book can be designed to meet the needs of those most interested.

What you want to know you ask on the questionnaire. The format most likely to be responded to will ask *2-5* questions, short and straightforward, each with a reply box to be marked. You might also leave room for additional comments. Ask them please to return this card by mail today! Thank them in the letter and on the questionnaire. And don't include a place for their name or address; if they wish, they will write that in.

Finally, if you use an index card, include a #9 return envelope with your name and address on the front. Put an actual stamp on both the return and the original mailing envelope—some say that several stamps will increase the response even more.

How do you test the price? Gently. One way is to give the respondent a choice of three different prices on the reply card. A far better way is to divide your test market into three equal groups, giving each group the same geographic spread. Then you send the same information sheet to each group except that one group has the book priced at X, the second at Y, and the third at Z. The latter approach will generally give a more accurate response if the test group is sufficiently large.

All that remains is to see if the positive replies exceed, equal, or fall short of the percentage of potential buying return you need to realize the kind of profit you want. If it exceeds or equals that percentage, charge ahead. If it falls short, you must find out why. Is it the test? The price? The subject? The book's contents? The timing?

If it falls far short, now is the best time to alter or abort the book, before hard work and hard cash come into play.

Do you run both tests at the same time?

Why not? Test other publishers to see if they will publish the book, when, what they will pay, and how well you and they can market your words.

And test the niche market to see if your targeted percent of those contacted will buy your book, at what cost, and what profits you might expect that way.

Then make a choice.

Two things are certain: you won't know about the standard publishers unless you ask, and you don't want to risk the high promotional costs of niche publishing until you have a solid sense of the likely buying ratio and rate.

Get to it!

Chapter 12

GATHERING INFORMATION AND WRITING THE BOOK

You've tested your idea and title one or two ways, the results are in, and you want to publish your own book—great! Now comes the real work.

At this step you must write a book that is worth far more than $19.95 to the buyer. To do that you must plan precisely what the book will say, figure out how and when you will gather its facts and quotes, set up a writing schedule you will adhere to, put the words on paper, have them proofed, and edit that prose into final form.

A recustomizing before you hunt for the words

In Chapter 6 you began the customizing process. Since then you have determined what promises the book must keep, given the work a title, devised a tentative table of contents, and brought the project into a distinct form.

Now the earlier steps must be further refined. Your purpose statement, necessarily general at that time, must be sharpened to match this book's specific topic. That will change the working question. The secondary questions will likewise become sharper.

Then a review of the books that you surveyed must be done again. You will want to study in depth those books that bear directly on your final topic. And you may have to search deeper and wider for additional information.

As you progress, fill in and adjust the outline from the table of contents. Determine how each chapter will be written, including:

(1) the order in which its facts, quotes, anecdotes, and other items will be used.
(2) the sources of those items: references, resources, own experiences or observations, etc.
(3) the kinds and sources of all illustrations

Determine the perspective, the angle, that you as the author will take in relation to the material and the reader. Are you an expert sharing expertise? An information gatherer and explainer? Is the material to be presented objectively or subjectively?

If your position is that of an expert, what must you do to reinforce or enhance the buyer's perception of your expertise? Join an association? Get licensed? Renew or update your license? Publish or speak to gain more, wider, or better exposure?

There are other ways to enhance you, your expertise, or your book. Would a foreword by an expert in the field help? Or co-authoring with a person with wider recognition? Sometimes a companion workbook lends value to the major text. And testimonials on the front or back cover, or both, can greatly add to a book's professional acceptability, as can testimonials on the flyer.

The role of illustrations and how they will be coordinated with the copy must be considered now. If illustrations are needed for your pages, are any of those that are used in other sources suitable and accessible? What will they cost? Will the rights' holder permit their use? Or can the illustrations be developed or purchased elsewhere or in another way? Where? When? Cost?

Finally, at every step you must continually ask, "Does this book satisfy the expectations of and the promises made to the buyer?"

Some very basic thoughts about getting information and starting to write your book

Very basic. Start by checking the key word of your topic in an encyclopedia. While you know some things about the topic, there are gaps to be filled. And since there are gaps, you don't know what you don't know. Thus, start from an assumption of zero knowledge, skim what you understand, search for rudimentary elements you never fully grasped plus anything else that is new, and work from the center outward.

This can be greatly enhanced by doing a Google search to see what is available digitally.

The digital catalog in the library is a great place to begin your hunt for written information. You've done much of this in Chapter 6. Go back again. Follow the numbering to the stacks to find other books that address your topic. Copy and investigate the bibliographies of the books that deal directly with your subject. Check again the *Subject Guide to Books in Print* and *Forthcoming Books*. Try different libraries: university, city, specialized. You can secure virtually any book in print through the interlibrary loan system (ask the reference librarian) or even buy used books inexpensively on the Internet.

Often a ton of good information hides in newspapers and magazines. Check periodical indexes; ask for the microfilm, microfiche, or old copies and dig in. Newspaper indexes are helpful. Remember that virtually every academic discipline also has its own index, each with hundreds of obscure journals listed.

I have found Robert Berkman's *Find It Fast* and Ellen Metter's *Facts in a Flash* quite useful, or check for other how-to-use-the-library guides to shorten the hunt. Ask the angels of the stacks, the reference librarians, for help, too.

As for interviews, there are books about the technique but little mystery. Know something about each person you wish to interview before you make the contact, know basically what you want from that interview, prepare your questions in a logical order, then ask. Interview in person or by phone. Seek permission before you tape, if you do. Tell the people why you are interviewing them.

Get to the point quickly; then let them talk. Finally, be accurate in quoting. If you don't understand something, ask for another explanation. If you miss a response, ask the informant to repeat it.

When you have enough library material (references) and live material (resources), convert that into copy. Arrange it in some order, match it to your outline, and begin typing. Don't worry about spelling or grammar, just get the material down. Work a section or a chapter at a time. Set a schedule and keep at it. Then ask what is missing for full comprehension or presentation. Get it and write it in.

Look at the order. Does it make sense? Does it flow well? Can the reader understand it? Move sections around, switch sentences, play with the text until it strikes the best balance. Then check spelling and grammar. Bingo, you have the first draft!

One way to record information

To write a book you need reliable information close at hand. Remember that books, like articles, are made from facts, quotes, and anecdotes. Often those come from widely scattered places: your computer, the library, the field, interviews. So you go to the information, take notes, bring them back, sort them, and keep writing. Let me suggest one way to record those notes that will bring you maximum return for the time invested.

First, though, what do you record them on? Some use legal pads, keeping the items on separate sheets by topic or source. Some just write things down in the order in which they occur or are found, also on legal pads. Others prefer to isolate each idea or point on 3" x 5" index cards. And others do one or all three on their laptop. (If you taped the interviews, they must be converted into written form.) Whatever format you use, you must clearly identify the origin of everything noted; that is, you must tie each point to its source. (If you are the source, write "me.")

It becomes tedious having to list the full source of each point made. So here's a way to simplify that. Say that you have five legal pads or five files in your computer. On the top of each pad or file you write one of the following: (1) facts, (2) references, (3) resources, (4) expert bio information, or (5) related topics.

Then every time you get a fact that you think is pertinent to your book, you write that fact on the (1) **fact** legal pad, file, or index card. If that came from a written source, the first time you use that source you draw up your (2) **reference** pad or file and you write down the full bibliographical information: author, title, publisher, place of publication, and date. You also give that written source its own letter, say "A." Then on the fact sheet, after the fact from that source, you also write "A" followed by the page number, say "A-17." (If there are several volumes, like an encyclopedia, you might list the volume too.) Thereafter, every time you use that same source you need only put its identifying letter and the page (and volume) number. At any future time you can instantly return to the origin of that written information to verify, recheck, whatever.

But let's say your source isn't written but oral: an interview, radio talk, tape, or speech. Again, the facts go on the fact sheet, file, or index card. But the source is noted on the (3) **resources** sheet, used here to mean oral resources. You simply note all that is needed to pin that fact back to its origin. Perhaps Ronn Owens' radio talk show, 11/23/07, 10-11, KGO, interview with Ivan Rasputin. And you give that a Roman numeral, say "II." (You must avoid the letters that are also commonly used Roman numerals: I, V, X, L, C, and M.) On the fact sheet you simply note II. Or if there is a series of interviews, on the fact sheet you note the Roman numeral and the date.

The (4) **expert bio information** pad or file is where you will build up a list and biography of those quoted or cited who are experts in the field of your research. Divide this pad alphabetically. Perhaps Dr. David Jones is an expert often quoted. Under "J" you will list his name, followed by every biographical fact you can gather each time he is cited or quoted (noting the source with the letter or Roman numeral). You can supplement this later, if necessary, from a current *Who's Who in (Music)* or similar library biographical listing. Why bother? Because at some point you may wish to interview this expert, for the book or spin-off articles, and this gives you a list of potential interviewees as well as information at hand about them.

And (5) **related topics** is where you note every spin-off idea, every new angle, every unique approach, anything that will let you expand your production and earnings from information gathered. Also, this is where you note other ways the information can be used: by other means, by combining means, and so on. One way to encourage the latter is to title pages on this pad by the other means: articles, seminars, speeches, audio CDs, consulting, etc. so that when you think of another way to use the information there is a place where it and like ideas can be noted.

Confusing? Too complex? Actually it's the other way around. Confining your note taking and record keeping to specific pads, files, or cards and tying all together by their sources—(2) references and (3) resources—does everything you want it to: provides information, sources, spin-off ideas, and additional biographical data, all at hand, together, and documented.

A writing schedule and tools

Figure out your publication date, subtract two or three months for the production phase, and you will know how many months you have to put words on paper. Then set a daily or regular quota, take the pledge, and get writing. Some measure their output in chapters (one a week, for example), in pages (2-5 a day), or in words (maybe 2,000-3,000). The important thing is to set a pace that can be maintained, then do just that.

As for your writing tools, that is left to your imagination. Ultimately, it goes on a computer_since you need the manuscript in final digital format. Why not start that way so you never have to make the transfer?

Some no less basic thoughts
about editing and proofing

There are three levels of editing. The first you do as you write, by moving words around mentally and on paper. This should be kept to a minimum. Think in simple sentences, put them down, and go on to the next thought. That way you can finish the first draft while you are still living.

When the first draft is completed, you must then go through the text word by word and make each word and phrase justify its existence. Be precise. Clarity and accuracy are essential. If you can't make your copy read clearly and correctly, you must hire someone who can.

At this point, if another firm was publishing your work, you would send this final draft for their further editing. But since you are self-publishing, you must hire a good editor/proofreader. However good you are, you need a second set of trained eyes.

Where do you find editors and proofreaders? Some are listed in the *Literary Market Place* and your telephone book. Some advertise in writers' magazines. Check with your local writers' clubs or organizations. Consider faculty in the English and journalism (communications) departments at local high schools or colleges. I've had good success with librarians. You can seek references from local publishers and the newspaper. Rates are also listed in the current *Writer's Market.*

As a self-publisher, you will have another person edit and proof your copy. Then you must correct the draft to prepare the final text for printing. Prudence says that when you are completely done, have a second proofer give it another, final reading.

Illustrations

The illustrations most commonly found in books are photographs, charts, graphs, line drawings, and other artwork, like cartoons. Study other books in your target field, then review the contents of your own book to see if illustrations are appropriate or needed.

Here's where you do the photo hunting. For example, let's say that your book tells how to play *pelota de guante*. While researching, you will want to check and note the credit of every photo you see about this Andean sport and, if you are in Quito, you may want to both take photos and get the name of local professional photographers that you may wish to hire.

Early on, you must determine precisely what you need, how the illustrations will be used, their approximate size, whether horizontal or vertical, and the paper on which they will be printed.

Even more important is whether they will be printed in black and white or color.

Photographer's Market is an excellent source for photos, photographers, and release information. Professional photographers at local stores, newspapers, and colleges add to the available pool of talent and information. For stock photos, also check stock photo information on the Internet.

As for drawings and graphics, local artists often serve quite well. Ask the local art club or league for names of the best. Graphic artists and advertising firms are another source. Sometimes students of art, journalism, or computer graphics can be hired or will serve an internship working on your book. Local ads often draw herds of cartoonists.

Self-publishers involving others in the illustration of their books might well avail themselves of *Publishing Contracts* by Dan Poynter and Charles Kent (www.parapublishing.com). These are sample agreements for publishers on CD, for easy downloading. Of particular interest here are (18) Release for Photographs and Illustrations, (19) Illustration and Artwork Agreement, and (20) Agreement for Paste Up, Layout, and Book Design.

Copyright and your book

Specific, free information about copyright, the process and costs, is available at www.loc.gov from the Copyright Office (Library of Congress, Washington, DC 20559). Simply download the TX form (or what you need) and follow the instructions.

I'm not a lawyer so if you need legal advice in this area you should seek it. But there is little mystery to copyrighting your book.

One, you want to register the copyright after your book has been printed. All the copyright does is prevent others from using the words (or charts, photos, etc.) as they appear. To do so they would need your permission. What you create is yours. That is, the words in the order in which an idea is expressed are yours. The idea, however, is anybody's. Others can restate that idea in their way, even similarly to yours. And they can use your words in other combinations.

Conversely, when you use others' words from copyrighted sources on your book's pages, you need their permission. Or you must significantly restate their ideas. (Note that government printed material is almost never copyrighted and thus can be reused at will.) You will also need permission for illustrations, unless they were produced for you on a work-for-hire basis. But words said to you in interviews do not need written or stated permission. Nor is anything stated in public protected.

Since the words are yours, their use by other means are also protected. For example, the rights to articles or a script are, like the book rights, yours to give or sell to others.

Permission to quote letter

If you use a significant amount of information directly from another source, in the same words or nearly so, you will want to have permission to do so signed and in your possession before your book is sent to the printer.

What is significant? I don't know and the courts aren't very clear. Titles have no copyright protection. Material written more than 110 years ago is almost certain to be in public domain. But just a word or two of a song or poem can be significant given the total number of words. Photos, cartoons, artwork, and several sentences or a paragraph or more from another's article or book also likely need a permission release. When in doubt, give credit and get permission—or express the idea in different words or in a different way.

How do you get that permission? The same way that others will seek it when they want to quote your book. The fictitious example below shows how a letter might look that I would receive requesting permission to use material from one of my books. It is very similar to a standard old model that was first shared by Herbert W. Bell in *How to Get Your Book Published*. Note that both segments are part of the same letter, in this case sent to me. The second copy is signed and returned when permission is granted.

DATE

Permissions Department
Communication Unlimited
P.O. Box 845
Novato, CA 94948

I am writing a trade book entitled *Entrepreneurs and the New Age,* to be published by Ajax Press. It will consist of approximately 220 pages and be priced at $17.95. I understand that the first printing will be 5,000 copies.

Identified below is material from one of your publications that I would like permission to include in my work, including any paperback, book club, Braille, large type, and foreign language editions or recordings, including electronic, of the work that may be made throughout the world.

A duplicate copy of this letter and a self-addressed, stamped envelope is enclosed for your convenience in replying. If permission is granted, please sign and return one copy of the letter, indicating on it how you would like the credit line to read.

Sincerely yours,

Budding Editor

MATERIAL TO BE USED:
From *Empire-Building by Writing and Speaking,* by Gordon Burgett, the title and full list on pages 9-10 (paper and cloth editions), "Fifteen Steps to Empire Building ... objective, means, and implementation."

Permission granted by:

Date:

Requested credit line:

Chapter 13

PRODUCING THE BOOK
OR HAVING IT PRODUCED

It's one thing to write a book; it's another and a far more complex thing to produce a book that you will show to colleagues and sell to peers.

On the surface, converting prose into serif text on numbered pages with captioned illustrations and chapter headings, a table of contents and index, the ISBN number secured and correctly placed, four colors on the cover, errorless, tasteful, and reeking of professionalism is enough to drop novices to their knees begging a New York house to keep at least 90% to "do it right!"

Even worse, it *is* about as confusing as it seems. And yet what you are building—the term is right—is, for all its stairwells and towers, no more complex than rolling up your sleeves and following steps, one by one, in a sensible order, doing personally what you can and letting a professional do the rest.

Fortunately, you've had the model of this product in your hand since first grade. A book is a book. Your task is to convert your knowledge into a peculiar kind of book eagerly sought by your targeted market. Still, it has a cover, pages, words, illustrations, and an order.

And you have another advantage: there are several excellent texts that will take you through the process, step-by-step. They are so good there is no reason for me to say inadequately in one chapter what they take many hundreds of pages to do right. So I will limit myself here to providing a list of particularly useful books, plus add some comments and a chart. They will explain book production.

Where to find help about self-publishing

I used one book to help me convert my ideas into publications. Since my first books were not niche targeted, but for the general writing and speaking public, this book was triply helpful for preparation, production, and promotion.

Dan Poynter's *The Self-Publishing Manual* has been repeatedly mentioned on these pages. I first used the 1979 version and have continued to consult each of the 14 revised printings for the newest names and addresses of services in the field. The book is chuck full of facts, guides, a production calendar, and examples.

Where the TCE approach differs

The Poynter book discusses self-publishing in the conventional sense and is excellent for general, small publishers, who are numerically in the vast majority today.

Niche Publishing suggests that there is a different way of publishing that can make books that are otherwise probably too marginal for conventional preparation and marketing nonetheless highly successful and profitable. This book also provides both framework and guidelines for the self-publisher serving a niche. The major difference is in the order in which things are done and how the specific needs of a particular buying audience are met.

Poynter suggests that the self-publisher creating a general book (1) writes (or has another write) the book, (2) produces the book, and (3) sells the book, pretty much in that order.

I propose that the publisher of a niche book (1) finds the target market first, defines what that market needs to read and couldn't resist buying if it were available, and identifies the selling requisites, then (2) writes (or has written) the book so it is in fact deservedly irresistible, and finally (3) produces that irresistibility for all to see. The actual selling of that book (4) is a simple extension of the first three.

Which means that when Poynter discusses preparation and promotion, what is said, all useful and applicable in its own context, must be sifted and weighed as to its value and order in the TCE process.

Yet what he says about production works fine for the niche book. So I send you Dan's way to learn how to produce your book, to absorb and follow and adapt, to turn out your own masterpiece, one that meets every requisite of your hungry market.

What is production?

Production is everything from putting the words into a final, corrected manuscript to turning out a finished book ready to sell. That also includes type selection and style, cover choice and binding, book design, bidding, layout, paper preference, illustrations, printing, and much more.

Who should do what?

Few folks are universally gifted, and of those even fewer have the time or interest to do all aspects of book production well.

What you can probably do better than others is the targeting, research, writing, general production coordination, sales marketing, promotion, and fulfillment. If not, move those items where you are deficient, disinterested, or short of time to the next paragraph.

You might seriously consider hiring others for the editing and proofreading, book design, cover design, artwork preparation, printing, and perhaps the flyer artwork.

It isn't easy to find such artisans with book preparation experience. The *Literary Market Place* is a place to start. Check other publishers. See if there are regional publishing associations or contact the Publishers Marketing Association (PMA) at www.pma-online.org for any source guidance it might offer. (It has an excellent monthly magazine for small publishers.) The telephone book is a first guide. Sometimes you can swap services with other publishers if you are proficient where the others are not.

A supplementary flow chart

While other books will show you what you need to know about book production, a simple flow chart might give your action better cohesion and direction. That is the purpose of the chart that follows.

In summary, while writing the book you must consider other production needs. Some texts require illustrations, which must be produced or bought. If you are using others' words or illustrations, you must also secure releases. And somewhere early on, the cover art must be done, including testimonials. Later, printers must be bid.

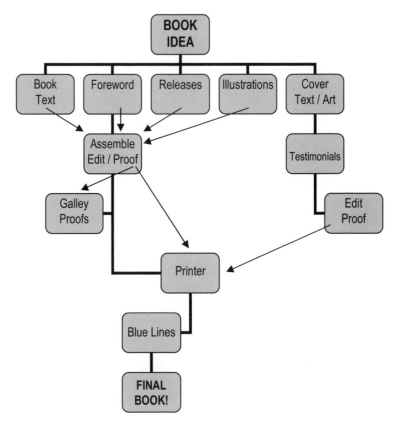

Two kinds of testimonials help sell books to niche (and most other) markets: short, laudatory comments on the cover(s) and in a foreword. They must be secured before the cover artwork is finalized or the book is printed.

The book is designed, pages are laid out, fonts are chosen, and the edited text is set on your computer. Illustrations are inserted and the book is proofed. The result, on disc, is sent to the printer, where it is joined with the cover sent by the graphics artist. The printer creates the plates (now paper plates), the "blues" (black on white) are sent with the cover proof, and you give your final okay or last-chance change. When approved, printing and shipping complete the production phase.

Some final thoughts about the above steps

(1) **Typesetting**. Today you can do everything needed on a PC or MAC, including the inclusion of .jpg photos. You may have to send it to the printer in some .pdf format, which is a simple conversion of the final draft into a universal platform so it will appear as you send it on the printer's machinery. A useful book here is Aaron Shepard's *Perfect Pages*, a short primer on using Microsoft for designing and laying out book pages.

(2) **Book design**. Find other books in your market, or elsewhere, that you want your book to look like. What kind and size of type? How big will the book be? Where will the numbers go? How will the chapter headings and sub-headings look? Will you use footnotes? There must be some consistent rationale. Either design it or get someone else to do so. Most important, the design must work for your market.

(3) **Printers.** Some time early in the process prepare a master bid and send it to the most likely short-run printers. Use the *Literary Market Place* for the most recent list.

Don't worry about bidding too early. If you bid on 204 pages and 50-pound paper and later want 220 pages and 60-pound, the printers will adjust the cost. Just send the same numbers to every printer in the first bid so you can compare. When you pick a winner, check recent customers to see if the printer met the quality and the book was delivered on time. If so, set up final dates for text and cover delivery.

(4) **Releases**. If you absolutely need or want to use something requiring a release, get it as early as possible. Releases should be in hand before the final copy is set. If there's a delay, you can set the copy two ways: with the text you want, approved, and/or rephrased or reworded, or simply deleted in case it doesn't arrive by the day the copy goes to the printer.

(5) **Illustrations**. These depend on three things: (1) how vital they are to the text, (2) if there is sufficient space, and (3) the kind of paper and press used. The first is the most important: are they a must to this market? If so, find space. But be certain that you make clear to each printer what you plan to include and the paper you will use. If high quality resolution is required, ask to see examples of what was done with similar work in the past. No surprises here.

(6) **Cover**. This will be either paper or cloth, to match your market's buying demands. If your buyers only buy cloth (hard cover), your book will be covered in cloth! But if you want to save buyers money and that is important, a trade paperback is what you need.

Use a four-color cover if your book will be sold primarily by bookstores, where an eye catcher of many colors is almost mandatory. If sold through a flyer, sharp, distinct colors that photograph and reproduce well in print are important. Often TCE books meet both criteria. But avoid putting reds and blacks next to each other: both are black to a b/w camera!

(7) **Binding**. Do what other books to your market do, unless there is some compelling reason. If your book is a cookbook or should lay flat to be read (like a typing textbook), use some comb for binding. Otherwise, Smyth-sewn or perfect bound are your usual choices.

(8) **Blue Lines**. The term is inappropriate today since these are no longer blue; rather, it's the book in almost-ready-to-go-form. This is the last chance to make changes or the book will appear as you see it in final print. Go over it very closely. Making changes at this stage costs time and money and can often result in a delayed printing, so much more attention should be paid to the final galleys before they are even sent to the printer. Blue lines are less important if you have no or few illustrations and you have inserted them properly. Do you need blue lines? Prudence says yes. But they raise the cost. If, for example, you are only concerned about a specific section of the book, get blue lines for that part only. (First book? Get blues.)

(9) **Book**. Some additional thoughts:

(a) If you want part of the books shipped elsewhere after printing and the printer is closer to them, have those books sent directly to that buyer, with the bill sent to you (or them).

(b) Consider shrink-wrapping each book. Costs 8-14 cents per unit but provides excellent shipping protection against moisture and scuffing. If sold in bulk, consider having two or three wrapped in each package. (But get more than half single wrapped.)

(c) Make certain the boxes are well padded and tightly packed at the printers, and check the whole shipment closely when it arrives, breaking into boxes at random to check for damage.

(d) Stipulate that every box should be marked clearly (title, paper or cloth, and box weight) for inventory control.

(e) If lifting is an issue, limit the box weight to, say, 40 or 45 pounds.

"If we value the pursuit of knowledge, we must be free to follow wherever that search may lead us. The free mind is not a barking dog, to be tethered on a ten-foot chain."

Adlai E. Stevenson, Jr. (1900-65)

Chapter 14

PRINT ON DEMAND
AND
NICHE PUBLISHING

The new variable in niche publishing is the ability to have a limited number of books digitally prepared and delivered quickly at a "bargain" price.

The process is called "print on demand." Rather than using the standard offset method that takes many nervous weeks going through the set-up, proofing, printing, and delivery, the print on demand (POD) process accepts what you send, puts the proof on the Web to review, and prints about as fast as the proof is okayed, arriving at your address in 3-5 days.

But it costs more per book and often the quality of the finished product (mostly the cover) is somewhat compromised. Also, there's nobody at the printing end to offer the sage advice (mostly about layout, paper, photos, and pagination) that "regular" printers often do if asked.

Let me share the three experiences I have had with POD. The first two involved Lightning Source (www.lightningsource.com). In the first instance, two years ago, we wanted to lay in a small stock (50 books) of *How to Plan a Great Second Life* in large (14-point) print. So we took the original 6" x 9" book and recreated it digitally in an 8¼" x 11" 216-page perfect bound book, which cost us $5.62 per book. (We used the same cover, stretched.) With the set-up charge and shipping, the final cost was a bit over $7 a book. Those sold for $22.95, so with our usual 55% discount to the middlefolk, we earned about $3 per sale—hardly a bonanza, more a side service simply to make a popular book available for those with sight difficulties.

In reflection, this was a general market book that was 90% sold through retail and to libraries, both routes heavily discounted. The niche publishing process described in this book didn't apply, which means that virtually none of the sales came directly to or through us, which would have increased our income to roughly $16 per book. (The promotion would have been included in the flyer selling the regular edition.) And we would have sold many, many more copies which, in turn, would have lowered the POD print costs or, most likely, would have made it possible to afford the slower but ultimately less expensive offset rates of our regular printers.

Thus, had this been a niche book on the TCE route, it is highly unlikely that POD would have been a serious consideration except in one instance: if by good fortune an order came in needing 20, 50, or 150 copies immediately (in publishing that means a week) and I had let the stock diminish below that number (one pays for that!), I would have contacted LSI (or another POD printer), cranked out the emergency stock (plus a few more to tide us over while the offset reprint was taking place).

Regarding quality, the book looked just like the offset copy would have, and the delivery was alarmingly fast.

The second book, let's call it ***Project Tree***, wasn't a niche item either, but rather a full book for general markets. I wanted it available in proofed form—with copyright, ISBN, and all—to distribute it to a group of potential sponsors and experts. So I ordered 20 copies, 6" x 9", 196 pages, perfect bound, for $3.94 a copy. Add $2 to each for the set-up and shipping, and it was a good deal: a private book that looked like an offset book, good quality, in my hands in a few days. But when this book reaches the public, soon, it will be printed in the thousands the regular way. And a particular offshoot book of the concept, definitely niche-directed and TCE-structured, will also need so many copies that POD will give way to the regular offset printers whose product, run in the thousands, costs dollars less even though it takes weeks longer to arrive.

Why even share these examples if they aren't niche published? Because you must know that POD exists, that there may indeed be times when having 10-50 early copies of a book you will later sell in the thousands will be hugely advantageous. And there may be wee spin-off books that will increase your offerings, expand others' perception of your expertise and spread in the field, and simply fatten (a bit) your coffers through add-on sales. LSI and most POD printers produce books from 48 pages up so POD must be considered there.

Another case where POD might work well is when your selling universe (target market) is quite small, what you are charging is sizable (15-30 times the cost comes to mind), and you don't want to print a warehouse full of books. You may be upgrading the book annually, plan to add new information to the book on a regular basis, or simply don't want to over-invest in the initial printing. Consider either POD or regular offset when creating your operating budget.

The third experience I can share began before the POD concept was in place. For years one of my prime products was a series of dental standard operating procedures manuals that were sold in large three-ring binders with a CD disc. There were about 10 such binders that varied in page content from 20 to almost 400, all printed on three-hole paper (actually the holes were drilled after the printing). Some books were printed on one side only, some had a mix of one- and two-sided printing, and some had sections printed in ivory paper mixed into the usual off white.[1]

In other words, no standard offset book printer could bid low enough to beat out the copy shops. Those became POD printers. We printed about 20 or 30 copies for each binder at a time. Was that a TCE project and niche published? You bet, a seven-figure

---

[1] This firm was recently sold to the books' author, Marsha Freeman. You can see the products at www.sops.com.

enterprise that today would be primarily POD based. So there is a place for POD in the TCE system after all!

Let me close with a few costs for you to consider, again from Lightning Source. To keep these current and find a dozen more firms eager to give you comparative numbers, Google "PODs" or check Poynter's list of POD printers in his book.

Using a 200-page 6" x 9" paperback, b/w interior, 4-color cover, with you digitally submitting the text and cover in ready-to-use format, you will pay for 10-49, $3.90 per book; 50-99, $3.71; 100-499, $3.32; 500-999, $2.93, and 1,000+, $2.73—all plus shipping. Check UPS ground for quick starting numbers there, calculating a pound a book. You will have to pay some printing set-up fees the first time too. These must be verified (since LSI regularly runs promotions) but they seem to be $50 for the digital cover file and 15 cents a page for the digital text file for each book (or ISBN).

In summary, POD can be a godsend, but it is usually too expensive per book for niche publishing. Test your market first, get a firm sense of the initial number of books you must stock, and if it is modest and your mark-up is high, look seriously at both printing processes.

Having said that, this book will assume you will be printing 1,000+ books and, for that, offset is the preferred way to go.

Chapter 15

PROMOTING AND SELLING THE BOOK

Done right, you promote and sell a TCE book from the moment you conceptualize it until the last copy leaves your warehouse or garage. The actual exchange of money for bound volumes is the natural conclusion of developing a product for a buyer that he/she wants and perceives as being the solution to a problem or a need.

How you let the buyer know that this invaluable object exists and can be bought is the focus of this chapter.

First, let me review the standard approach to selling a book. You will use some of those means. More important, you must know how and why the TCE approach differs.

Then I will discuss how to use those standard promotional tools to increase your book sales. Knowing how to prepare your flyer, then how to distribute it, is critical. Finally, assuming that all this promotional whirl creates sales, you'll need some ideas about filling orders—"fulfillment" in the trade.

The standard approach to selling a book

The standard approach presumes that most books will be sold through bookstores and that widespread interest can be created through general newspaper reviews, radio and TV talk shows, and other public means of advertising. Secondarily, it focuses on the library market, again encouraging review by major library magazines as a way to bring the book to the attention of the acquisition librarian. Also encouraged is direct mailing to book reviewers, bookstores, and librarians.

Since bookstores and libraries often buy through their own distributors or fulfillment sources, it behooves a publisher to also court those intermediates to get them both to handle and "push" the book.

But almost all of this approach directly conflicts with the TCE method because success in the latter comes from having identified a specific market at the outset, customized your book to meet its very needs, and then expanded from that base. Which means that only a small percentage of the public is likely to buy your book, although a high percentage of the niche fraction will. So a selling campaign that depends upon the book being selected by the public at large would be, for you, excessively expensive for too small a yield.

More specifically, if your niche market is bakers or ice fishermen or criminal lawyers, it is unlikely that either general bookstores or libraries will be very interested in stocking or displaying your wares. Yet there is always the possibility that your book is slanted in such a way that both its targeted market and the broader populace might find areas of common interest, so at least libraries and perhaps bookstores may wish to add your book to their offerings. Some of these standard selling means might be selectively pursued. First, though, concentrate on getting your book in the hands of your niche market. They are eager to devour its pages. That will fill your purse.

Using standard promotional tools
for a TCE book

To sell a TCE book massively, fliers work best. One of every four books is sold by mail, and the tighter yours is directed to its niche and the better your flyer is, the better your chances are of earning $50,000+ this way. Best yet, the responses are fast: a reliable figure finds half of those who will respond do so in four weeks, 98% in 13. Still, anything that informs your niche market of the book's existence and desirability and makes it available for purchase should be investigated and probably pursued.

So let's quickly look at the standard promotional tools first, then discuss the flyer later, in greater detail. Some of the standard promotional means are more important to TCE sales than others. Let's discuss them in a rough, descending order of importance.

Testimonials, for starters. In every field there are people whose opinion others value. You want their opinions in your book, on its back cover, or in your flyer. There are two times when that is best sought. One, when the book is in the drafting stage. You might ask people to technically or critically review a chapter or two. Ask for a general testimonial at the same time. The second time is from the galley proofs or when the book is about to be sent to the printer; you can send a copy and ask for a short testimonial. Not all will say yes, some will want to wait until later, some will never reply, but, surprisingly, many will send you the blessed affirmation.

Do testimonials sell books? You bet. They help get better book reviews too. Another valuable kind of testimonial comes from satisfied buyers. These are usually letters. In all cases you should get the words in writing and ask for permission to use those words promotionally. It's also best to use the person's full name (rather than initials), occupation, and (if possible or relevant), age, and city of residence.

Testimonials are particularly valuable for TCE books. In niche markets the sphere of acquaintances is usually smaller, the luminaries better known, and anybody else in the profession or field recommending the book can catapult it into a much better selling position.

Book reviews are even more valuable, if they are positive and appear in key magazines or journals read by your niche market. They can result in many thousands of books sold. The key here is positioning. Brain surgeons or lepidopterists, for example, aren't likely to read and rush out to buy a book in their field that is reviewed in the *National Enquirer.* But in their own technical journals, yes. That's where they expect to find such reviews. Good words by a peer on the right pages make all the difference.

Dan Poynter and John Kremer (in ***1001 Ways to Market Your Book)*** will tell you how to get books reviewed. They will also tell you how to get your book listed in the major directories: ***Books in Print***, the Library of Congress indexes, *Publishers Weekly,* and library journals (if library sales are a possibility).

Other than a favorable book review, the most important standard promotional tool is an **article** in those selected publications most read by your targeted market. An article that you write should either come from the book or relate to the information discussed in your book. It can be a direct excerpt. Usually it will be part or all of a chapter reworded for magazine use. The material is yours to use; you can update it, add details magazine readers want to know, insert quotes culled for the article only, or expand the text to more closely fit those readers' needs. Very important: in your by-line it should say that the material comes from your book, with the book's full title, publication date, your URL and street address, and the purchase price.

When a magazine or journal pays for articles, you win twice! Others will use the article and consider your bio plug your payment. Don't quibble: just being on those pages is worth gold—if the article is good!

Book clubs are ideal ways to get widespread publicity and approval all at once, though *per se* they are not very lucrative. Many fields have their own book clubs, as the *Literary Market Place* indicates. They should be approached when the book is in the rough draft to galley stages since the club will want to buy the text when it is first printed. A significant order can pay for all of your printing—their copies and yours—so your sole expense would be the promotional cost of your copies. The rest is profit. The bonus? You print in big letters on every book: BOOK CLUB TOP CHOICE (or whatever is appropriate)!

Card decks are often sent to specific markets and your book might well be promoted on such a card. Again, the Standard Rate and Data Services publications list card deck firms by markets served. Talk to others whose cards were in the most recent mailing to see if this might work for you.

If those in your niche market attend conventions or regional gatherings, a **display booth** might be considered. Not only could a giant reproduction of the book cover be shown, the actual book itself should be at hand to be touched and reviewed, and fliers could be given to every passer-by.

The best of all worlds would be for a firm to use your book as a **premium**, buying it in lot from you and distributing it to some or all of your niche market. That requires a promotion of a different sort, to interest firms in your product as a premium. Poynter and Kremer touch this.

You might distribute your fliers as part of a **larger mailing**, perhaps with other, similar books or even other products of direct interest to the target market. Seek the most prestigious group dealing with your target market and suggest an insert. You can shine by having your book promoted in a flyer inserted, say, in a magazine. That also sells books! Check the same SRDS publication that discusses card decks for information about insert programs.

Sometimes **display advertising** in journals and newsletters that serve your target market is worth the cost. (Place your own ad through a second company name and save the 15% commission; pay in cash and save 2% more.) Before that, as the book is being printed, send press releases to any publication that might be remotely interested whether or not you plan to advertise in them later. The release should describe the book's contents and you as its author.

Classified ads might also work. If your niche market turns to specific classifieds, put an ad where they look. Don't list it under "book" unless they are accustomed to seeking items by that title. Better to list it by topic. Nor should you mention the price, which is too high to justify in so few words. Get people to go to your website to seek more information. At the website, you can sell it directly, with a discount or other enticement to get them to your ORDER page. Your response will include an irresistible flyer about your book, plus anything you offered to get them to write. (You also have their names for your mailing list whether they buy or not.) How do you get them to respond? Offer a teaser: "Ten ways to ... " Ten ways they need to know. Ten ways that lead to your book, which is the best way to do what the teaser suggests.

Or it might include more information about all or some of the ten ways on its pages.

Speeches or **seminars** are seldom thought of as promotional tools, but they are exceptionally effective ways to sell your book. Not only can you make it available after the presentation (better yet, have the sponsor buy enough copies to give one free to every participant), the fact that you are speaking about the subject shows your expertise for having written about it. (Which is ironic since you often get the bookings because you wrote about it!)

Radio and TV may help, if your niche market watches or listens and you don't have to water down the subject too much to explain it to the average audience, thus making your knowledge and the book's content appear too elementary.

Are there **catalogs** serving your targeted market? Is your book included? Are there commissioned reps who sell to your most likely buyers? Are they selling your book? Does your niche market have an association? Does it sell products? Yours? Does it sell your book in its bookstore? You must put the same sharp skills you used in writing your book to making certain that those in your niche market find out about you and your book(s). Promotional and selling possibilities abound. Make every one of them tools for putting your words before the right eyes—at your price!

Anything that displays your expertise in your subject should help sell more books. Yet you will sell many more books much faster to that market if they are aware of the book's existence beforehand. The best way to do that, in your case, is to begin with a dandy flyer.

Preparing your flyer

Earlier you identified what must appear on this flyer: the benefits, the needs the book would meet, why a book was needed, and so on. You may have actually designed a dummy flyer.

Now review that material from Chapter 9, and the information sheet you sent to test the market in Chapter 11, and do the following:

(1) Make the content changes necessary to describe your actual book and its benefits. Study your target and secondary markets closely. Will the same flyer work for all? Do you need different fliers or approaches for different segments? How must they differ for each?

(2) Study closely every aspect of as many other fliers to your primary market as you can get. This is your competition, if not to sell a book at least to draw money from your market. How professional do they look? How many colors? Expensive paper? Are they stamped or do they bear the indicia? Include a mail-back envelope? Website-focused? Postage paid? Contain artwork and illustrations? Such details can save you much and earn you more.

(3) Convert the benefits and needs into copy that will best appeal to your primary market. Determine the illustrations and artwork needed to produce a competitive flyer.

(4) If you need a graphic artist to design and produce your flyer, select the best available within your budget. (Where do you find one? Ask other publishers for recommendations, check the telephone directory, consider a student in graphic arts as an intern to create your flyer under faculty supervision.) Look at other work that person has designed for your target market or about books.

(5) If you design and produce your own flyer, go to it. Most book fliers include a photo of the book, its table of contents, something about your expertise or the expertise of others cited, a money-back guarantee, testimonials, and selling copy.

(6) Discuss your final design, paper, and how to best use the illustrations with a printer who produces in the volume range you need. Determine a kind of paper, the weight, and how the illustrations will be reproduced. From that information prepare a bid from several printers. Select one printer and emphasize the need for the fliers on the promised date. Have the fliers printed.

Distributing the flyer

Now that you have the flyer planned or actually in hand, you must figure out the most effective yet least expensive way to put that flyer in the hands of your niche market. You must learn about direct mail.

Books are written about direct mail. This isn't one of them. I will remind you here of the key steps plus some critical concerns. Just know that using the mail as a selling means is expensive, risky, and somewhat uncontrollable. But it can also bring you the best results fastest by getting your niched message precisely where you want it to go. For the TCE concept it is simply the very best primary means of promotion.

The two most important elements: the mailing list and the mailer

Mailing list: You are already aware of accessible mailing lists to your targeted market, but there are several other considerations that come into play: their availability (quantity and delivery date), cost, method of addressing, frequency of cleaning, source, date compiled, discount if placed through your in house brokerage, and restrictions.

(1) Ask each list broker for particulars about their list. The SRDS mailing list publication already contains much of this information. You probably want a list that is current, just cleaned, and available in a few days sent electronically to your mail house. An active list compiled from products or services bought is better than one compiled from directories or otherwise indirectly gathered. Best if the cost is low, the list can be ordered in installments (nth selections non-repeating), and you can take the discount (deduct the commission).

(2) Determine when you will mail and how many names you will send at a time. Will you test a sampling first? What is the minimum number the list broker will let you test? Or will you mail to geographic sections? Will you mail twice to the same

list, renting at a considerable reduction those second names with the first? Will you send different fliers to different levels of the list? All of this should be planned before you order lists.
(3) Order the best list or lists available.

Mailing: The question is whether you will do this yourself or will use a mailing house to coordinate all of the steps. I have found that for up to 1,000 I can save money by applying pressure-sensitive labels and handling our own bulk mailing in-house. But beyond that it is more economical to use a mailing house. Naturally you will want to check the rates of all the local houses. (You can find them listed in the telephone directory, by asking others who use direct mailing, or by calling the local Chamber of Commerce.)

(1) After selecting the house you will use, let them see your mailer early in the process. At issue are its size, weight, open space for the address, folding, and use of indicia or a stamp.
(2) In some states if the printing is delivered directly to the mailing house, it is exempt from state tax. Check that and act accordingly.
(3) Almost all lists are sent to be printed by ink jet but if there is anything unusual about your request or the list you should tell the list broker. You simply have the electronic lists sent directly to the mailer, usually in a day or two.
(4) In fact, you can have the mailing house order the lists for you. The advantage? If the wrong list is sent, or sent incorrectly, and you gave the mailing house the right information (in writing), they must correct the problem. And they have the clout to do it faster and better. They don't charge for this service since they are paid a commission by the mail list broker.
(5) If you use a bulk rate indicia instead of stamps, you can usually use that of the mailing house and save the $175 annual fee.
(6) The major problem with mailers: getting your items sent the day you want them to go. This requires coordination between you, the printer, the list provider, and the mailing house. Let them suggest the best times so they will perform as you wish.

Mailing bought books is fulfillment

Once you have a flyer and the means to mail it, all that is left is to take the plunge, keep yourself busy for the next few days, then tend to the results. Which means fulfillment: getting those books back to the buyers as quickly as you can in first-rate condition, with a flyer, of course, that tells about other, related products and services you also offer!

Setting up a shipping department is the inevitable result of publishing a fast-selling book. Yet it needn't be a major headache nor entail extraordinary expenses. Simply set aside a large table, put the necessary items nearby, and either assign the task to some lucky employee or hire a part-timer to perform this function. It is ideal for your kids, somebody else's kids, or seniors. But they must be responsible and attentive; frequent praise and small raises work well here. Whoever does the job may need a car with a trunk to cart packages to the post office. The load is heaviest after you send your mailings and diminishes rather quickly between promotions. What follows are some quick tips that should save time and cost.

(1) You need a mailing address so buyers can reach you. An office or P.O. box are best at first since the post office may refuse to deliver to your home if the response is too large. Check with your postmaster.

(2) The books must be wrapped well to reach buyers in good condition. We use Tyvek reinforced envelopes for regular customers and Jiffy bags or well padded boxes for bookstores or others who will resell the goods. An invoice is inserted for the resales, while fliers plus any receipts (for credit card purchases) go into the customer's package. Both are then sealed securely and taped. A company address label goes on top. We buy Tyveks from Quill (www.quillcorp.com) and Jiffy bags locally from a paper wholesaler; we use our book boxes and some from behind the liquor store to send out quantity purchases, and buy labels (plus most office items except stationery) from NEBS (www.nebs.com).

(3) Books are mailed one of three ways. PRIORITY (when the customer insists and pays the difference), MEDIA MAIL

(least expensive but rudely treated by the Post Office), and LIBRARY RATE (to libraries!). The Post Office will give you or send you to their website for a rate sheet that explains all. Buy a hand stamp that says MEDIA MAIL since almost all of your books (or tapes) will be mailed that way.

(4) We simply buy sheets of stamps, tear them up, and mix and match. Stamp machines are fine but expensive and time-consuming. Get a receipt for tax purposes each time you buy the stamps.

(5) Very, very few books fail to arrive. If someone complains, we ask them to wait five more days and if it still isn't there, let us know. If it doesn't arrive, we send another. If the order to individual clients tops $50, we insure the package for its market value closest to $50 or $100. We ship larger orders to resellers by UPS.

(6) Record every order on a daily tabulation sheet You must account for the total income received: the amount for the book, product, or service; tax, and shipping. Accounts receivable are noted twice: on an A/R sheet when the invoice is typed and sent and on the daily tab sheet when it is paid. The figures on the daily tabulation sheet are then recorded on the income ledger, which we keep by the computer. Ultimately, the orders, some with credit card receipts, are attached to this sheet and filed should we need to consult any order or the daily tally at some future date.

(7) Keep complete books. You must account for all income and all expenses. Go to a stationery store and buy a general business ledger book. Modify it to meet your needs. You will need an ACCOUNTS RECEIVABLE and INVENTORY section. Or use an accounting software system like Quicken. But you still must keep all paper receipts and all orders.

(8) As mentioned earlier, unless you are doing business solely in your name—the Tom Smith Company (and you are Tom Smith)—you will need to file a fictitious business statement. Check with the county clerk for details. This must be done before you can open a business bank account.

(9) Visit several banks to check rates and services. Important will be the cost and availability of a Mastercard/VISA service through that bank since many customers will want to buy a

book that way. This will be even more important when you have several books or products. We now use a shopping cart system and link it to Pay Pal. That allows us to process more cards quicker and is perceived as being more secure by the buyer. Both services together cost about $50 a month.

(10) If you are in a state with a sales tax, you will need to register with the state sales tax office to get a resale number. Ask any other businessperson who sells products for the address: they are painfully aware of their local taxing group. Be modest in your estimate of the sales you will make at the outset or you may be required to post a bond and pay more frequently than other new businesses. Check locally to see if other licenses are required.

(11) You need a federal tax number only when you hire employees other than your family. Otherwise you report the business on your tax form as a sole proprietorship or partnership.

(12) Keep the full name, title, firm, and address of everybody who inquires by phone (if possible) and by mail. You may not get that for email orders, but at least get the email addresses. Those will comprise your future mailing list. When you write a second book to this targeted market, you send a pre-publication special to those names or email addresses so they can order at a discounted rate before the book is available to the public. This can result in the printing costs being met before anyone has read a word!

EXPANDING

The "E" of TCE means "Expanded"

If your niche market will buy your information in book form to meet a need or solve a problem, why wouldn't they buy that same information by other means? Or more or similar information in another book by you?

Would they pay to attend a seminar to hear more about your topic? Would somebody or some firm or association pay you to give a speech about it? Or could you sell books or other products to those coming to a seminar or speech?

Would they hire you as a consultant, to learn how to apply your information to their personal or corporate needs? Would they buy more information through a newsletter as it becomes available? Would they rather hear the book on audio CDs as they drive? Or see you explain its main points on a video or podcast?

Again, what you are selling is expertise. Why sell it once in one form only? Why not take the information gathered while writing your book and share it many ways?

For example, as we saw in Chapter 7, why not produce articles, consult, and offer seminars from the information gathered as you write the book? And from the seminars develop both speeches and tapes? The book, in final form, would yield more articles, and further gathering of related information would provide a basis for a newsletter. The book, in turn, could be sold at the seminars and speeches as well as through consulting and a newsletter.

Expansion from a common information root allows you to multiply manifold both income and exposure, which in turn enhances your position and perception as an expert. It is also far easier and less expensive per item to sell collectively many products by direct marketing to a specific buyership.

Expansion is the reward you get for doing the targeting and customizing right. The rewards can be huge!

"The best way to become acquainted with a subject is to write a book about it."

Benjamin Disraeli (1804-81)

Chapter 16

CONVERTING THE BOOK INTO MORE BOOKS

Once you have written a book you have a core from which many more books can be developed. We set an earlier goal of earning $50,000 from your first book and suggested that you could probably earn another $50,000, or much more, by expanding from that information base. In this section we will focus on that second $50,000, or more, through additional books. In the next section, through other means.

The spin-off books can be new editions of the original book (changed, updated, or both), they can come from further development of elements introduced in the first (or subsequent) book(s), or they can be books about closely related topics of interest to the same niche market.

Each successive book is easier to research (you know the sources), easier to produce (you know the process), and easier to sell (you know the buyers).

Best of all, easier to sell. People want more good things from the same good writer. Which is why your first book must be excellent. And why it makes huge sense to go to that same well time and again.

Here are 12 ways to turn your first book into many more. (This list isn't definitive. Find other ways that apply to your topic and knowledge.)

(1) The most obvious: every three years or so you go back to the same book, update and expand it, include new quotes, review new research, and add new sources to the bibliography.

(2) Write a time-dated book: *Optometrists: How to Save 50% on Your 2008 Income Tax*. Next year is 2009, and so on… See examples of tax prep books in the bookstore. But it needn't be taxes. It can be computers, where to find current cancer research, the National League pennant race, and much, much more.

(3) Write a many-pronged book. *Five Things Every Successful CPA Needs to Know*. That's the first book. Each of those five things is the core of the next five books.

(4) Write the follow-up to the many-pronged book, also many-pronged. *Ten More Things Crucial to Successful Accounting*. And, you guessed it, each of those ten is the core of the next ten books.

(5) Focus on stages of importance to the targeted market, beginning with any stage and filling out the cycle with subsequent books. An example of such a cycle: (a) *How to Form Your Own Band*, (b) *How to Double the Number and Value of Paid Gigs*, (c) *How to Multiply Your Band Income Through Product Sales*, (d) *How to Get Your Band Recorded, Played, and Rich!*, (e) *How to Take Your Band National!*

(6) Having become identified with a core topic by writing about it, gather all the other writing about that or directly-related topics and prepare an anthology. Most of this writing will already be in print as articles, reports, or studies. Additional material could be prepared by you or others in the field specifically for this anthology. You are the editor; if you also contribute, you are both editor and a co-author (with one or many).

(7) Produce a book of comic relief. Unless you are extraordinarily gifted in a comedic way, this will be an anthology of jokes, cartoons, quips, anecdotes, humorous excerpts, whatever makes the niche market laugh. These can be gift books for those in the field to give each other or for those outside the field to give to the insiders. In the latter case, your marketing must be expanded and approached differently.

(8) Use case studies for books. A book could be one case study or a dozen clustered around the same point or theme. These could

also be produced in booklet rather than book form. You could write them, co-author, or publish the case studies of others.

(9) A source book is a natural since you are already familiar with the main texts and how the targeted market might use additional information. Such a book is really an extended, annotated bibliography plus a listing of all additional resources: experts, agencies, speakers in the field, key college or university departments, current research and researchers, money sources, etc. The contents must be accurate and current. Conduct a computer data search. Those are particularly salable if the information and sources are problem/solution based.

(10) A how-to, step-by-step action guidebook which addresses one problem and provides one or various solutions. This would be a good match to a more general first book that broadly covers the field.

(11) Here you can use virtually any of the previous ten but alter the targeted market and the related facts, where appropriate. There are topics where the basic information is roughly the same whether given to a salesperson, a minister, a welder, or a piccolo player. Even the presentation format requires little change. So here you find what is different for the new targeted market, adjust and verify those changes, and produce a book either about the original topic or to deviations like those suggested. All examples used would pertain to the new target buyers.

(12) In this spin-off category you zero in on the buyers of your first book. You have their attention and many of their names; you know how to order and use their mailing list. So here you ask what other need do they have that is as pressing as that chosen for your first book. Then you write a book about that new need. If they have many pressing needs, you have many potential books—or one or several books about various needs. Given the opportunity, I would respond both to the urgency of the need and its proximity to your first topic, moving from that most closely related to the first book to that least related, attempting to build on the expertise displayed about the topic in that first book.

Incidentally, you needn't write all or any of the spin-off books. Rather, you can use your knowledge of the buying market and the prestige of having written the first book to become a publisher for those who follow. Publishers run the greatest risk but earn the lion's share of the profits. Writer/publishers earn even more.

There are two main points to add regarding book expansion. The first: since you have established your expertise with your niche market about a particular subject, you build from that strength, moving slowly outward and deeper so that everything you do further enhances that perceived expertise. The second: you focus on a pattern or process and you apply that to many markets. From *Lawyers: How to Maximize Your Earning Potential* to *Doctors: ..., Faculty: ..., Truck Drivers: ....*

Of the two, the first will almost always be less risky and more profitable. It is simply easier to sell one person many good things than many people one good thing. The main difference, to your coffers, is the greater ease and lower cost of promotion.

Chapter 17

SHARING THE INFORMATION BY OTHER DISSEMINATION MEANS

Not everybody wants to read a book, and not all information is best conveyed that way. Teaching the movement of a particular ballet, for example, might be done on paper, but video is better. Martin Luther King's speeches read well; seen or heard, they gain immense strength and they teach more. Interactive seminars defy capture on paper; the medium is molded while the information is shared.

So the question here is how the core of your book can be shared again, as is or restructured, by other means of dissemination. How it can be remarketed through articles, speeches, seminars, CDs, a newsletter, consulting....

Moreover, how you can reap even higher profits from research now completed and expertise established in a tested target market.

The concept and process of taking information and forming and packaging it profitably by many means would take a full book to explain well—and I actually did discuss this in two earlier books, *Empire-Building by Writing and Speaking* and *Niche Marketing for Writers, Speakers, and Entrepreneurs*. But let me share three basic steps now by which you might expand your book into other means:

(1) Complete a fact chart about the subject and means.

(2) Identify the most appropriate means and prioritize those to create action paths.

(3) Extract, again prioritize, and put into a time frame those actions most likely to earn the highest profit. From that, develop an action plan.

Let's invent a book and a wee action plan to better show what I mean.

Let's start with a simple title but a not-so-simple book: ***How to Create a Million-Dollar Restaurant from Almost Nothing.*** (No, I have no idea how to do this, but there are hundreds or thousands of potential book writers who do.)

Here is my other means action plan.

It starts with your book as its core, with an expected $50,000 profit from it.

Within a year I would publish one of two companion books, either (1) a case study book with detailed, replicable, actual examples of restaurants that followed your example or served as the bases of your information or (2) a much more detailed, step-by-step, numbers and layouts, menus and more workbook that will help the reader of your book (long on theory) put that theory into brick-and-*maitre de* action. I would expect to earn another $35-40,000 from that book.

Its time factors appeal to me. Figuring the first book at 8-10 months to complete, about 6-8 months for the second, you can also write related articles and give speeches during that 18-month period as well, in part to help finance the books and your modest empire. (Mind you, you're not building restaurants, too, but focusing on explaining the process.)

Why articles? Because they fall into your lap as you write the book and they tell enough of your story to get the readers to want to buy the book mentioned in your bio tag (which tells of you, the book[s], and your website where they can be bought). They are great publicity and may even pay you a few bucks ($100-250 or more), but even just having them in print free is a great reward. Expect to sell 5-300 of your books from a good article. (I once sold 800 in two weeks.) Shoot for six articles, one every three months.

And parse out the core of your concept, focus on three solid examples (leaving the critical details in your book[s]), and get booked to speak to restaurant or wanna-be restaurant audiences, figuring five such talks bringing from $500-2,000 each. Let's say $5,500 in total.

And round out your action plan with consulting. Figure spending $200 getting the stationery, phones, and answering service/machine. You will consult about what you wrote, mostly helping the serious apply your process. If you start at $100/hour (moving up as the demand exceeds your time), let's think of another $25,000 from this source, particularly when both books are out, for the two-year action plan's phase one.

How much would this bring in gross income (almost all of it profit)? $118,600.

Action Plan / Phase One		
Book 1	$50,000	profit
Book 2	37,500	profit
Articles	600	+ books sold
Speeches	5,500	+ books sold
Consulting	25,000	

This isn't the book to walk you through each of these actions, beyond explaining the initial book process (and, by extension, the second book). The bibliography will help some. But paths are paths and I think it makes a bundle of cents to plan one and develop it as much as you can while you are creating your core book.

Still, because they are possible doesn't always mean they are for everyone. There are eight variables that you must consider when you convert an action path into an integrated action plan:

(1) your interest, available time, and energy
(2) how it fits into your general life goals
(3) your risk tolerance: none *guarantees* any income at all!
(4) your financial resources and their accessibility for use now
(5) the cost of each element—time and expenses—for each means

(6) the success of your initial book
(7) the interest of your niche market in using the means, plus its ability and desire to pay for the product or service, and
(8) the availability of the information you wish to share

A last thought

There is no such thing as totally safe publishing. It's always a gamble. But there are ways to make sharing of information through a book safer, more profitable, less bewildering, and much more helpful to people who desperately need your help. That's what I've tried to share with you on these pages. We need to know what you have to say. And you should be rewarded for saying it. So go to it! Think small to grow big!

Chapter 18

THE LONG TAIL
AND
NICHE PUBLISHING

I'm hardly a believer in divine surprises but it was odd that the very day I mailed the text of this book away to get proofed I somehow stumbled on Chris Anderson's book *The Long Tail.*[1]

Odder yet, I have no recollection where or when I first saw it referenced.

I was headed to the library to return a thriller-killer and in my run-around box (mostly for post office mail) sat a fragment of paper on which I had printed the title and author. So I slipped my book into the return box and walked over to the digital catalog to see if any library in Marin County, or even in California, had heard of *The Long Tail.* Unbelievably, it was on the stacks less than 100 feet away, complete with stains and smells of a taco that had been spilled on page 95.

I read it, laughed and shook my head about twenty times, and knew from the third page that I had to tack on another chapter to share it with you. Why? Because Anderson gives the big picture from a new view about where we fit in that mystical world of niching—and how it is changing.

It seems that what I think of as tightly-targeted (or niched) he sees as endless, and where I see a bounty for publishers (enhance-

---

[1] Chris Anderson, *The Long Tail*: *Why the Future of Business Is Selling Less of More* (New York: Hyperion, 2006).

able through empire building) he sees as potential profits once the path of distribution is unclogged and the products' existence is known through the Internet.

The Long Tail?

What's this book telling us? That in the '70s and '80s, all we saw were blockbusters. There may have been 100 available movies to show, but there were only so many theaters to show them in, so we only saw hits.

And there may have been 100,000 music tracks available somewhere, but they weren't in your local record store, and almost none of them were on *The Hit Parade* or in the Top 100.

Only so many of those tracks could fit on the radio in a 24-hour day. Only so many TV shows on six channels.

And books, 50,000 may have been printed each year but only 7,000 reached the town store, and many of those stayed forever, like dictionaries, atlases, and the Bible.

It was a time of scarcity.

"What's new?" you ask. "There's still only two major wholesalers for books. You don't get through that bottleneck, nobody sees your words in the stores." True, but Anderson provides hope.

What Anderson does is see data with new and better eyes. And while he says that he didn't discover the theme or invent its name, his book provides the first clear framework for identifying and analyzing this revolutionary real-world phenomena.

It shifts the future focus from hits to niches. While hit books and movies and songs will be with us forever, Anderson shows that it's from the near-hits and almost all of the rest of the items in descending order, if measured by sales, that big money will flow. Or as the venture capitalist Kevin Laws says, "The biggest money is in the smallest sales."[2]

Anderson, editor of *Wired*, says, "If the twentieth-century entertainment industry was about *hits*, the twenty-first will be equally about *niches*."[3]

---

[2] Ibid, 23.
[3] Ibid, 16.

Why? Because by dramatically lowering the costs of supply and demand, the kind of buyers and the nature of the market also dramatically change.

The Long Tail explains that three forces are replacing scarcity with abundance: (1) the democratization of the tools of production, (2) the democratization of the tools of distribution, and (3) the connection of supply and demand.

I laughed when I read that because my own publishing proves his first point. The final draft in my first book, in 1982, was produced on a Selectric typewriter and the printing plates were set in lead. The finals of the second book were coded and fed into an electronic typesetter because my new computer had no proportional type. The third was done the same way because my printer was 300 dpi and I was told that plates could only be made from pages run on a printer that was 600 dpi or higher. The fourth book (and a dozen more) I set myself in Word and then cut and pasted the finals from copy provided from a friend's new 600 dpi printer. The last 60 or so books have been written and formatted on our office PCs, digitally proofed 2,000 miles way, finalized, then attached it to an email and sent another 2,200 miles to the printer, where they were united with their covers, also digitally transmitted.

In other words, in one lifetime (in fact, in less than 50 years) the tools are in our hands to create what we want: books, albums, movies, podcasts, music… That's the democratization of production. Every step faster, better, and cheaper.

But that does little good for those who don't produce hits, or don't even aim to reach the mass market top, if the explosion in creative output can't reach potential buyers.

The Internet is the greatest means of realizing (2), the democratization of the tools of distribution.

How did the Internet level the field? Before, extensive promotion could bring one movie to a million people, but the Internet, free, can bring a million people to one movie—or book.

No longer are niche producers ignored, or stopped from showing their wares because there is only so much shelf space or room in the catalog. No longer are they ignored because the push of demand from the stores requests only the top 5% of the available products.

The Internet is nearly limitless in what it can show, and thus make available, to buyers in every part of the globe. Ask Amazon, eBay, Google, iTunes, Netflix... If the largest bookstores hold 175,000 books and there are now 1,500,000 books in existence, the Internet end-around today makes it possible for every one of those books to be seen and bought.

That's where "the long tail" comes in. The third force, connecting supply and demand, drives business from hits to niches. It makes the search to find niche products instant and almost free. Not only does the word spread through Google, blogs, and best seller niche lists, it provides a believable sorting screen with others' reviews and recommendations.

For example, let's say you chart the sales of all books for a specific year using a standard format like this:

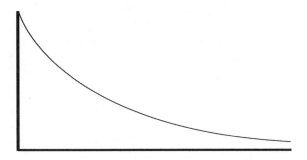

The hits are on the left (in the head); they may bring in half of the sales income. The near-misses are found near the vertical decline sloping to the right. What Anderson shows is that the rest of the sales, continuing to the right (forming the tail), will extend almost as far right as published books are available before the sales reach zero. That's the discovery: if there were buyable products, unimpaired distribution, and a wide awareness of their existence, the tail of sales never seems to end. A "long tail" in fact.

For example, a quarter of Amazon's sales come from items listed after the first 100,000 titles. And as the three forces gain traction, the tails in those firms that are Internet driven are getting bigger, longer, and more visible. Says Anderson, "The onesies and twosies were still only selling in small numbers, but there were so, so *many* of them that in the aggregate they added up to a big business."[4]

The undeveloped or suppressed pull for niche items was hidden behind the hits. Who knew the latent demand was there until the hurdles of distribution were removed and the awareness of the products was made universal?

Anderson shows that 98% of the music tracks were bought without regard to the number that was available. Many were hits, to be sure, but that 98% also included tracks in newly found categories like ambient house, a cappella, and Australian-South Pacific—never to be found when all you could do was buy in the store.

Proof? When scarcity was removed, the true shape of demand emerged and we got Amazon and Netflix. And when hits began to slow down, "where the economics of traditional retail ran out of steam, the economics of online retail kept going."[5]

How does that affect us?

The last words in this book (before this chapter!) were to "think small to grow big," after having suggested the thought process and tools to do just that. Anderson's book's subtitle is "Why the Future of Business Is Selling Less of More," and he shows why that is also true and how that concept turns the world of marketing upside down.

Or, in our case, rightside up. What it says to us is that the freeing up of distribution and the infinitely larger dissemination of the availability of our niche products, plus how they can be easily and quickly created by us and attained by buyers, will make anything of true value that we produce and put in usable, accessible formats much more likely to be bought or at least seen and considered by those who would most benefit.

Niche Publishing encourages the use of direct mail, an expensive, yet, if tested, low-risk way of linking your idea to those most benefited. Anderson, in our terms, is talking about almost every-

---

[4] Ibid, 9.
[5] Ibid.

thing else that will affect our extended sales. In the long run, the new relationships defined in *The Long Tail* might well lead to the creation of a different first-step process that would replace, or parallel, direct mail.

To make more sense of this and to share with you the new hope for nichers brought by Anderson, let me suggest two assignments.

First, read *The Long Tail*. It will strengthen your sense that having valuable information is valuable in itself, and that there is a system coming that will facilitate the just exchange of that information—if you do your part. That's to get quickly to the core of your message, unwrap it right, give it a just price, and be honest at every step in its creation, explanation, amplification, and even modification. Then let others know that you and your message exist!

In other words, take heart that today's inequities of distribution and promotion may at least be lessened because there is lost profit in maintaining the status quo. That your selling can't be stunted or stopped. That by using all of what you can now, and adding to that the far greater exposure you can and will get through the Internet, you can be properly rewarded and buyers can also be much better informed and helped.

Second, do what you know to do now to sell your book or product and seriously broaden your knowledge about all of the ways you can expand your contacts and sales through the Internet. As this book is written, Internet sales are just beginning to significantly increase the publisher's bottom line. But the time may come when that will be greatly enhanced for those of us in the long tail never destined to appear on general buyers' hit lists or best seller rolls, lest they be in our niche.

My book shares some straightforward advice: find something of critical worth to a specific, identifiable market; research it thoroughly; write clearly and illustrate fully (if needed), and, with your words, help those in that market solve a problem or do something better that desperately needs to be done. It suggests testing the market first to see if its potential buyers will pay for your solution or improvement. If so, then use direct mail as the tested means to let every person or firm most benefited know of your existence and what you have to sell. And the book proposes moving out from successfully solving problems for your nichefolk, expanding your solutions or improvements to related topics and/or by other information means. That's the empire-building that can indeed create a lifetime of secure, well-deserved income from buyers who reward champions in their field.

Niche Publishing and *The Long Tail* walk a common trail. We are its everyday foot traffic, you and me, wandering somewhere in the middle of the economic forest. It's easy to get lost, and easier to get discouraged, when there's no way to see above or beyond the trees. But Anderson offers a grander vision and says to forget the occasional giants on the trail with their fat money bags, that there's a better future for those of us seeking or serving specific niche tribes with our peculiar but no-less-important goods.

Let's go a step farther. Let's get our goods together now, so when there's more light, we are ready to more fruitfully sow and reap. In the meantime, while we are waiting, let's jump to the front of our niches and get our own empires flourishing!

**"Think like a wise man but communicate
in the language of the people."**

William Butler Yeats (1865-1939)

A CASE STUDY

Even though you've read lots of pages of how-to niche publish information, you still have little proof or assurance that the TCE process works—if you do.

I can assure you that it does, at least every time I've tried it (in 25+ years of publishing). One of our products, for dentists (with a spin-off for doctors) has grossed almost $2,000,000. Our three newest products, in the education field, work every bit as well (and we hope as profitably), and I've yet to see the process applied by others, when done as explained, where the risks of production weren't significantly reduced and the sales dramatically increased.

But let me walk you through a case study where I was the publisher of a book written by three of the top educators in the State of Illinois so you can see, with actual examples, how and why the process works as well whether you are the author/publisher or you publish others' works. I'll approach this study following the 18 chapter topics, and will try to align the explanations so they expand the steps and directives of those chapters.

The book in question is *What Every Superintendent and Principal Needs to Know: School Leadership for the Real World*, by Jim Rosborg, Max McGee, and Jim Burgett. (I'm also the oldest brother of that last author, lest the odd-name similarity confuse you.)

The book is directed to K-12 school administrators, but it could as well have been to any other niche field—whalers, career coaches, banjo players, or models—because almost all niche-marketed books follow a path very similar to that explained in this case study, with only the content of the selling tools (and the book itself) differing substantially.

Why have I chosen this book for this case study? One, it's both current (we just published the second, updated edition a few months back) and it has a few years of salability (the first edition saw buying light about 3½ years ago). Two, because the authors have agreed to my sharing the process and the numbers with you. Three, it's an easy-to-grasp example that developed in a classical, straightforward fashion, despite some minor procedural errors on my part. Four, because it's a success in progress. (Alas, niche publishing failures are usually quite obvious in the initial testing phase so the full book production process is aborted at that stage.)

The Case Study book's origin

In early 2002, brother Jim mentioned that he and two of his cohorts in education, Jim Rosborg and Max McGee,[1] were thinking of writing a book "from the trenches" that contained practical, everyday advice for their school superintendent colleagues, as well as for school principals. (All three were then superintendents and had been principals.) He knew that I had written *Publishing to Niche Markets* and asked if I could offer any advice about getting started and what to do next.

Clearly, theirs would be a niche book so I suggested that they (1) write the book and sell it to a publisher that worked the education field or (2) they collectively self-publish it. I also explained the gist of the TCE process. Using it, for a small testing cost they could see whether the intended market would buy their book before they wrote and heavily promoted it.

All three were at the top of their careers then, already working 10 hours a day in key positions, so they asked me if I would do that test for them, for a fee. Like them, I was far too busy writing and publishing books between speaking engagements, but, to my own surprise, I heard myself agreeing to do it! Even more astonishing, I told them that if the test was promising, I might be interested in becoming the publisher if they didn't want to perform that function themselves. But in either case, yes, I'd need certain information from them, and I would share the results and they could make the decision about whether to proceed or how, once they knew that made sense—and cents.

[1] See their impressive credentials at the website at www.superintendents-and-principals.com.

I agreed to do the test because, frankly, the test itself is not overly complex or time-consuming, they would pay the cost, and I was curious to see the results.

But agreeing to publish in a field new to me (though I had been a university dean and taught at every level years earlier) was a giant step out of my range of comfort. My offer wasn't done willy-nilly or precipitously. Which brings us to the first ten or so chapters of this book.

The premise

I knew my brother Jim and trusted him implicitly. In truth and competence he's the real thing. I asked him about the other two authors, and he said they were the best straight-shooters he knew or he wouldn't co-author with them. The three wanted to draw from their almost 100 years of combined experience to help other superintendents and principals create the absolute best districts and schools possible. And each of them specialized in complementary areas and they could provide four chapters apiece, plus a case studies chapter at the end.

"Will your education colleagues pay to buy your brilliance?" I asked Jim. He replied that school leaders are always seeking reliable and applicable advice so, yes, they or the school would gladly pay.

Thus the premise, "if you know something that others will pay to know, they will pay to know it many ways and by many means," seemed solid to me, at least as it applied to a book. I was also interested in whether the book would bring me enough profit to merit my effort and topic diversion. And I wanted to see if the authors would also reap enough reward from the time spent researching, writing, and rewriting the book, assuming that the royalties alone would scarcely be enough. (The usual royalty would be about 10% divided by three: I offered them 5% each of the net retail price, half of that on books sold for less than 50%.)

All three are well established in the higher education field, so a book would certainly solidify that standing among their peers and, by extension, make it easier to secure promotions or other honors. (From the outset I am presuming the book will be solid in content, properly lauded, and professional in appearance.) They were also established speakers in the trade, so I asked if the book would lead to enough future speaking presentations (figuring an income of $1,000-2,000 per program) to justify their writing it, when combined with the royalties and other spin-off income. They thought it would. I also offered them a 40% discount on books to sell back of the room or related to those presentations, which in some cases could double their income.

Publishing through a standard publisher

The choice of publishing approaches and firms was theirs, of course, but from my perspective it wasn't sensible that they would go a general market publisher.

That choice would require preparing a full book proposal (often taking many months) and sending it either to one or many publishers for review—or to an agent (after finding one who would represent them) who would do the same thing. Acceptance would be the first, high hurdle, followed by writing the book, checking the galleys, and waiting the usual 18 months or so before it was released.

It would probably take two years to reach their public and would lack any specific target marketing, particularly an early test to see if anybody would really buy it. Rather, their book would be one of 12 or 145 released by that firm that year to find its way to their colleagues' hands. Risky and very slow business.

Using niche publishing

For all of the reasons outlined in this book, I assumed they would niche publish the book, unless they encountered a standard publisher with successful books similar to theirs, strong placement in the education market, and a quick book production record. The latter was unlikely (as you will see) so I didn't dally here, expecting that if I didn't follow the TCE process and publish it, they would do it themselves (which, they admitted, was highly unlikely) or find another niche publisher, firm, or person to do it for them.

Finding, defining, and qualifying
the target market

After assuring myself that the authors were capable of providing quality information of top value to their market—although whether they would do so in a timely manner, and later would be willing and able to handle the edited rewriting, was an unknown,—I needed to see the size of the selling universe so I could guesstimate my potential income.

They defined the target market in their original request as K-12 superintendents and principals. I added to that board of education members, honchos above superintendent at the state and national level, and instructors offering college classes to school administrators. I divided those into two groups by the way they would be marketed: (1) direct mail and (2) other. Only the actual superintendents and principals are in the first group, and my hard calculations are made from them. Income from the rest would be a much appreciated blessing.

Could I find the first two, as defined, on current, accessible, affordable mailing lists? Yes.

If I used a quick test for qualifying the most likely buying universe (using the first group only, since the rest were hard to calculate or were less likely buyers), would our book be worth pursuing financially?

To do that I looked at books being sold to K-12 administrators that were similar in style and purpose and noted their length and price. Although none was the same as what they proposed, those closest ran from $14.95 to $50+, so I set three initial check prices, at $ 17.95, $19.95, and $24.95. (If each chapter was 20 pages long in a 6" x 9" format and there were 13 chapters and a bibliography, index, and front matter, I calculated our book at approximately 300 pages. Books that size cost $19.95 and up, with most in the $20-30 range.)

Then I used my TCE formula that said if I sold to 10% of the mailed-to market and it cost me one half of the cost of the book for production and promotion, and I had to pay 15% of the retail price for royalties, would the remaining money justify my taking the time, effort, and risk to publish this book?

In 2002, there were 901 superintendents (45 regional/856 district) in Illinois and 16,836 (with mailing addresses we could contact) in the rest of the U.S., for a total of 17,737. The number of school principals found 3,583 in Illinois and 105,558 elsewhere, for 109,141 nationwide. So I used those numbers in my calculations.

Multiplying those by 10% at the respective prices (the direct mail buy rate), dividing by two (for profit level), and subtracting 15% of the respective retail price gave me these totals:

> **At $19.95** (rounded to $20)

SUPERINTENDENTS

17,737 x 10% = 1,774 x $20 x 50% = $17,740 - 1,774 x $20 x 15% = **$12,418**

PRINCIPALS

109,141 x 10% = 10,914 x $20 x 50% = $109,140 − 10,914 x $20 x15% = **$76,398**

> **At $24.95** (rounded to $25)

SUPERINTENDENTS

17,737 x 10% = 1,774 x $25 x 50% = $22,175 - 1,774 x $25 x 15% = **$15,522**

PRINCIPALS

109,141 x 10% = 10,914 x $25 x 50% = $136,425 − 10,914 x $25 x 15% = **$95,497**

Thus, my publisher's profit, very roughly calculated, would be $88,816 for a $20 book and $111,049 for a $25 book—if the buying ratio and profit percentage held.

That's a huge "if," but the calculations must start somewhere, and in niche publishing we can conduct a quick and relatively inexpensive test to see if such a buying appetite exists and if, in fact, we can produce and promote for 50% of the gross income (minus the royalties later). You will see the test we conducted a few pages hence.

(These figures are from direct mail marketing sales only. I will use some of my "profits" to market the books other ways, which should result in more sales, more income, and more profits.)

It's not enough, however, to have identified a market large enough to create potential profits. The folks in that market also have to have the money and desire to buy the product, plus be contactable by mail at a fixed address. We mentioned that earlier: the money is there for a $20-25 book, and the desire to improve their schools certainly will justify that expenditure. Their presence on the mailing lists assures their reachability.

My conclusion: the authors have identified a niche market, the buyers are qualified, there are enough of them, and we can specifically reach them by job title if not by name, so let's move to the next step: does it meet their needs?

Finding and defining a specific market need

This was the first question I asked Jim, Max, and Jim. "Why would your peers read what you have to say?" Granted, they are nice guys and each has a cadre of friends, plus family, but once all of them have bought a copy (hard to sell a copy to your mother), why would the rest of the academic leaders buy another book when their desks are piled high with them, unread?

Their answer was what a publisher wants to hear. They were going to address, in detail (with current and verifiable facts), the 12 most pressing areas that affected superintendents and principals. Moreover, all three of them had come up the ranks—from teacher to principal to superintendent (Max McGee had even been the Illinois State Superintendent of Education)—and each knew where the pains were and are, plus the remedies to alleviate those pains.

I was convinced.

Then a whiff of good fortune interceded: I was headed to St. Louis to speak and if the three could meet me there for an afternoon to discuss the project in detail, I would meet the other two and we could talk about the feasibility of squeezing four and a third chapters out of their busy schedules in a timely fashion, if we could all get on the same page about the purpose, structure, and marketability of the book.

We met and I discovered that brother Jim's friends were as down-to-earth and flat-out funny as he was, which promised, if not some levity on the pages, at least a comfortable working relationship in the book's creation.

We also spoke of their future plans—lots of speaking, consulting, and articles beyond their academic duties—and how those would help us (and them individually) sell more books through sponsoring associations, districts, and organizations.

So would their book meet needs sufficiently important and central to the target market that it would be reviewed, featured, chosen as a text for grad education programs, and bought? Yes.

Meeting that need through a book

But is a book the right way to go? Has someone else written a book similar to this one? Is it on the market, or about to be released? And if we create a working question, secondary questions, a table of contents, and design the book's contents, is there enough honest, needed information to fill its pages?

I started this research the easy way: I asked the authors. All agreed that there was nothing like their book on the market and there was more than enough to fill 200-300 pages of content that they would certainly have bought whenever it had been available.

But there's nothing worse than a dumb surprise to upset your niche publishing dreams, so, while I trusted the three, I headed to the computer and library and reviewed all of the current books then available for superintendents and principals—lots of them.

And I checked *Forthcoming Books* to see if just such a surprise was within six months of seeing publication light. Nothing.

Was a book the best way to share this information? I mentally ran through the dozen or so other means of information dissemination and only speeches, seminars, or workshops seemed as likely to draw the potential buyers' attention (and cash). The authors were all capable of giving those very presentations, and wouldn't a book both draw participants to them and/or be a logical purchase at or after them? I liked the synergy and felt the book of the choices was the better lead item. They could give the speeches, sell my book and earn a discounted difference to increase their (and my) income, and the book would still sell in a thousand locales the speeches didn't reach.

All that was left was the mechanical part of defining precisely what need(s) the book would meet, reduce it to a working question, ask the secondary questions, create a table of contents, and give this book form and legs.

So I asked the authors to send me a list of the chapters each proposed writing and the order in which they suggested they appear. To that we added a final chapter of short case studies. I would add in the rest: introduction, index, etc.

I was a bit alarmed when I saw the chapter list—it was extremely comprehensive. What title would fit so many topics? Let's answer that a bit later.

What they provided convinced me that, with tweaking, a winner book was just waiting to be born. And a book was the best starting means.

Meeting that need through other means?

Other than the speaking means just mentioned, which would be initiated by and to the profit of each of the authors, I didn't dwell long here. Simply, the authors wanted to publish a book and might use it later to enhance their speaking income but they were far too busy to entertain other means at that time. And so was I, frankly.

Still, I had to consider three other items: (1) a digital book, (2) digital chapters, and (3) a website.

Once the book had been created, edited, proofed, and given final approval, it was ready to send by email to the ink-on-paper printer. (The cover would be sent separately, digitally, by disc, FTP, or as an email attachment.) Joining that digital material together, I'd have the core of the same book that I could sell as a digital download. By adding a new ISBN number for each digital format and converting the slightly modified contents to be reproducible in that format, I'd have another product that I could sell, directly or through ebook sellers like lightningsource.com or amazon.com, whenever I wished. (In fact, a digital book can be on the market days or weeks *before* the printed book leaves the press.)

And, if there are buyers for a whole book composed of 13 independent chapters, would there be buyers who would purchase those chapters alone? Perhaps instructors eager to add them to a class syllabus, other authors using them in an anthology, or individuals needing only that information?

This is also when a website must be considered, if not earlier, to get the best URL as its address. Since it costs less than $25 to reserve a name on the Internet where book buyers will logically go to seek the book, I wrote down a dozen possible site names, and asked the authors for their suggestions. Since the book was still without a title, what I chose was www.superintendents-and-principals.com. (A strong case can be made for not using the hyphens. Alas, that site was being used then.) My choice included the titles of our target audience, the user wouldn't have a sense of being sent elsewhere to some unknown location, and if we later decided to do more books to this audience, it was broad enough to include them and any other related products.[2]

Why a website? Marketing today is strongly web-centric. Buyers expect you to have an address that they can access freely where there will be more information about you, your products, or whatever else it is that you are doing. Which is precisely what you want them to do. You want them to inquire, at which time you can

---

[2] Which is precisely what happened when the same three authors wrote and I published **The Perfect School** in 2007. And it served as an ideal cross-reference location when Jim Burgett wrote and I published **Teachers Change Lives 24/7** that same year, though I used as its primary website www.teacherschangelives.com.

tell them more about the book, the stellar benefits its purchase will bring, a chapter or two to read, and what others think of the book. They can also learn more about the other products or services you provide, review the authors' credentials, and have a quick, easy way to safely order and buy whatever they wish (while leaving enough information to be included in your in-house mailing list.)

So I will focus on the book here (in printed and digital form) as I secure a URL and set up the shell of a website at my server.

But if this had been a sole venture with me the writer and publisher (as most of my books have been), this is when I would have spent much more time and attention designing an empire, deciding precisely which means in what order would be developed before, during, and after the book's creation and development.

(I did create the digital download version in .pdf format within a month of the book's release and the first edition sold very modestly [under 2% of the total books sold, at $20 each] by us and others. There was much less interest in purchasing individual chapters. Six buyers wanted them in digital form, all to add to class anthologies. So that was discontinued for the second, 2007 edition, although we will permit it if instructors or buyers contact us directly with the request. And, as mentioned, the website created was www.superintendents-and-principals.com.)

Where and how will I sell these books?

An early question I had for the authors was where they bought or how they heard about books specifically directed to superintendents and principals. Most heard about them from peers or saw them at gatherings, read reviews in their professional journals, or received information by mail (less often, on the Internet). A few saw them in libraries, and almost none first saw them in bookstores.

So putting books in those locations will be my first priority.

Another obvious sales outlet was at the presentations given by the authors, either in arrangement with the programmer to provide a book to each listener, at a back-of-the-room (BOR) display at the presentation, or by mail later.

The fastest (though not least expensive) way to get a needed book in front of the most responsive eyes is through an eye- and mind-grabbing flyer addressed and mailed to them or to the position they hold.

That is why we are testing this book for direct mail selling. Fortunately, both the quick study numbers and the test mailing returns (as you will soon see) indicate that a healthy return can be expected by adhering to that as the book's primary marketing mode.

But I also expect there to be a healthy number of additional sales from the website, at gatherings of superintendents and principals (like district or regional study days, conferences, and conventions), libraries, other promotions or sales by the authors, to school bookstores for use as a textbook, and perhaps by businesses that deal with academic administrators.

Much farther down the list would be bookstores, like Barnes and Noble and Borders, though both have solid education sections. (Since these books are sold to the wholesaler at a 55% discount, both our profit and the authors' half royalties cannot survive alone on the occasional education administrator finding and buying these books from their shelves.) The same for Amazon.com, where we must offer the 55% discount plus pay the shipping. Presence there is more to establish the book's existence than to reap a livable return.

What about selling extensively through the Internet—ebooks, user groups, links at every possible site, high placement on google.com, ads to capture roaming book hunters, and so on? I have read the writings of the high-power proponents of this "new" series of interrelated venues (and the promises of six-figure certainty) but I'm sufficiently unconvinced (and uncertain) that superintendents and principals have enough time and energy to seek reliable school-related information this way. And if they aren't noodling around the computer looking for what we offer, I'm not going to waste my time and energy making information available where they aren't. So I will limit my presence to the website to being caught by the search engine spiders, offering digital download versions of the book, and keeping a mailing list of our website buyers for some future use, until I see proof from other niche publishers that I'm wrong. (But my mind is open to the use of blogs and podcasts in the near future, if I can see how they will directly or indirectly bring back three times the cost of their production.)

Or through book clubs? Good idea, arranged at the first printing, but I couldn't find one for this narrow a niche.

Later, as the book appears (and slightly before, in galley form, for library journals) I will increase the book's visibility through the many means of promotion. I will particularly focus on getting complimentary copies to the top leaders in the field plus every key publication, journal, and newsletter so it can be promptly reviewed. (A few of these contacts will be done many weeks before the final printing, to get some short, positive testimonials to use on the back of the book and the selling flyer. They will be sent complete or partial galleys or directed to the book-in-progress file at our website so they know what the book says and how it is structured. In our case, this was easier because the authors already knew most of the leading luminaries.)

The purpose here is create a rough selling plan so that the marketing is done in the most logical order. Yet we will begin listing book and author information on the website months in advance of the actual release, and posting free chapters to read in advance as soon as they are edited and proofed. We will also offer a 10% (or even 20%) pre-publication "SALE" on all orders received before a set date (usually the date of release). And we will contact any of the selling links in advance (particularly book clubs) to offer a discount on to-be-printed books, in part so that they can be sent directly from our Midwest printer without having to be shipped through us in California. Finally, we set up the paperwork to get them listed at the wholesaler, bookstores, and Amazon.com so they are listed and available almost from the first day.

(My guesswork in 2003, above, had about the right selling order [seen from 2007], with one surprising modification. One of the authors had worked extensively with a large bond underwriting firm, and they felt that the book would be a valuable gift for K-12 top administrators. That resulted in the sale of about 1,800 copies of a special printing, substantially discounted. We never saw the book, other than two proofs. It went straight from the printer to the buyer!)

The book's promises and promotional tools

Up to now we have been qualifying our book by defining and quantifying its target market, the needs our book will meet for that market, seeing if other books exist (or soon will), asking if a book is the best lead product, and guesstimating which selling methods and markets would work best. But we haven't written the book nor have we invested more than a few dollars in the project. We still don't know if, however brilliant the concept, anybody will really shell out money to read its pages!

So, on the path to conducting a modest test to see if this is a worthy investment, we must begin to hone in on the tools we need for that test.

Of all the information needed, nothing is more important than determining what promises you will make on the back of the book, the selling flyer, and the test flyer.

This is where we artfully imply reward, advancement, happiness, promotion, more money, and security while we tell why it is imperative that they read and do what the book says. We must tell the truth, the book must do what it promises, and the text must be written so it can be easily understood and applied.

Fortunately, *What Every Superintendent and Principal Needs to Know* says it all in the title (though we didn't have the title yet!). That was precisely the aim of the 12 chapters plus one, so my task as the publisher was to make sure that potential buyers knew what the contents were and then, as the editor, to pound out any pedantic puffery or murky meanderings in the promo (and later the text) into practical, working prose usable by the brightest and dimmest bulbs in the arena.

The best way to get to the core was to create a few right-on paragraphs and a table of contents around which we would build a test flyer that would be sent to a small portion of the buying universe. I asked the authors for a couple of summary paragraphs, since I already had the contents, and then I reworked what they emailed me and injected some humor—we agreed that the book needed a fair portion of honest laughter to keep the readers reading. We came up with these three items:

Finally, 256 pages of no-nonsense, usually funny, always honest ideas and techniques from three of Illinois' top administrators—for the price of a two-patty burger deal and a movie!

You will laugh from front to back but the book's intent is deadly serious: to propel you, your school, and your system straight to the top.

Why your board should buy this book for every administrator in your district—

The authors are three guys who rose to the top in school administration because, under fire, they could provide practical, successful solutions to almost any predicament. Even more, they could innovate, cut through the jargon and nonsense, and lead. So on these pages they share what they have learned: ideas, high-impact lessons about leadership, and everyday problem solving that can be immediately implemented at every school level. Their combined wisdom and stories will make administrators think, laugh, and act.

Table of Contents

1. School Leadership
2. Civic Leadership
3. Business Leadership
4. Communications
5. Trust
6. Planning
7. Expert Knowledge
8. Building Internal Capacity for Success
9. Expanding District Boundaries
10. Supporting Successful Teaching and
    Learning
11. Adventure in Innovation
12. Taking Care of You

You'll notice that I forgot to include the case studies—a dumb oversight since more people in the past three years seem to have read the case studies than any other single chapter! And that we first thought the book would be about 260 pages, which is 256 because it divides by 16 (web press books are cheaper that way). But you must start somewhere when the test book is still an idea on paper.

This is not the first draft. I sent that to the authors and each had his way with it. They trembled at the humor, so I reduced it (a bit). A few chapter titles (really summaries because they had to fit in a small box) were slightly reworded. It ended up as you just read.

All that was missing from the test flyer was a title, short biographies of the authors (no room for photos, and who cares?), a book cover or facsimile, a SATISFACTION GUARANTEED box, and the details: kind of cover, price, book size, ISBN number, availability date, and a website for more information.

Good promises to build from…

A title and testing tools

Nothing is more important to a niche book than its title.[3]

I appealed to the authors for a good title or title and sub-title. It was, after all, their book and they had to be proud of it. But the titles they suggested were duller than sandstone, obtuse, so broad that we could have parked a tank under the covers, or just not appealing. Said another way, I wasn't going to publish a book using any of them!

---

[3] For a general market book that would be "its title and cover," but for niche books, while the cover must look professional and the back cover must help coax the browser to look inside, all the buyer will see of the cover is a much reduced copy on the mailing flyer. If the flyer will be printed in color, then bright, catching colors are indeed important, but if it's to be in black and white, then too many dark colors will make the print hard or impossible to read.

I mulled over this dilemma for a day or two, and in the process asked myself, "What does this book contain?" An immediate mental reply was "what every superintendent and principal needs to know." There was the title—they agreed, after a bit of prodding. (I hurried to the computer to see if anybody had beaten me to it!) Still, each had a favorite subtitle, and one was pushed with undue vigor, so it appears on both editions, alas in much smaller type: School Leadership for the Real World. It made sense and, who knows, maybe thousands bought the book because of it.

Did I test this book to see if larger, general publishers would be interested in it, assuming that if they were I was on much stronger financial ground doing it myself? I never even considered it. It takes too long, general publishers sell poorly (if at all) to niche markets, and by this time I could see a solid buying public whose coins I wanted.

So I must now create the rest of the tools to conduct a wee sample test I had earlier explained to the authors. I'm still not fully committed to publishing the book at this point, and they have the option of going elsewhere after the test results are in, so the last step in our agreement before that publishing decision is to find a mailing list and put together a test flyer, test note, and reply post card to send to them.

Here was the original scheme for the test study that I sent to the authors:

It would consist of two actual mailings. I'd order 500 PS (pressure-sensitive, peel-off and press) labels, nth-selection (the total list divided by 500 and produced in ZIP order) from the best education mailing list house, and divide the sheets sent, figuratively, into two piles. The second pile would be the 248 labels not sent in the first mailing. All 500 would be sent the same flyer, postcard, and letter, but testing prices would vary in each mailing. We would begin by printing 500 copies of the letter since that wouldn't change and didn't include the book price.

The next two items, the postcard and flyer, would list a book price, but in all other ways would be identical. Let's say that we set $17.95 as the minimum price worth the effort, but we also think this book might be bought at

$19.95 and $24.95. (The best way to guesstimate this is to see the price at which other, similar books are currently selling.)

So, for the first mailing to 252, eighty-four (84) addresses would receive a flyer/postcard saying the book costs $17.95. They are the A group. Another 84 would get information with $19.95 as the price—the B group. And the C group's info would say $24.95. Then we'd put A material in 84 envelopes, B in 84, and C in 84. We'd take the PS label sheets and the first label would go on an A envelope, the second on B, the third on C, and then we'd leave three on the page before the seventh again goes on A, the eighth on B, and so on. The envelopes would then be sealed and mailed. As long as our list is in ZIP order, that way we'd have the As, Bs, and Cs spread evenly across the U.S.

Most of those replying, from my experience, do so within about 10 days. We'd determine the minimum percentage response that is acceptable, and if that is met by one or several of the prices, we would use the remaining 248 labels to second-test the most favorable response, plus a test price above it.

Say that $19.95 shows the biggest return. We would then divide those 248 remaining labels into two piles. Again, all would receive the same letter. But here 124 would have the $19.95 price on the post card and flyer (they are the D group), and the remaining 124 would have the price at $24.95 (the E group). Of the remaining labels, the first unused would be D, the next E, followed by D-E-D-E, etc. until they are all labeled, then sent.

All things equal, we would determine the book's final price from the results of both tests, plus see if there is sufficient income from that selling venue to make it a profitable venture. We'd also look at other venues that would expand our marketing and the authors' related exposure.

I told the authors they'd need to help me produce the three items we were testing—the letter, the postcard, and the flyer.

We put our heads together to create the flyer, which reduces what the potential buyer knows about the book to one page: title, contents, some bio slots of each author, benefits, type of book, a guesstimate of the pages, an ISBN number (which I provided), and anything else they suggested, all readable on an 8 ½ x 11 sheet of paper, one side.

This is where caution and hard thinking must occur because the only thing that the test respondents would know about the book was on this single page. We were investing several hundred dollars to see if those recipients (as models for all school administrators) would pay "x" dollars and would in fact buy the promises and information they read on the flyer. If we totally blew it, we might use the 248 names left to test, instead, a new book title and contents, but that was risky business. So the first flyer had to be the best we could do.

The Flyer

The actual flyer appears on the next page. It is larger and clearer at www.superintendents-and-principals.com/flyer1.htm.

Alas, this flyer didn't just fall from heaven in final form. Let's share some of the concerns the four of us discussed before it reached its final, one-page format.

Most important was the title. If that doesn't "grab" the buyer and state quickly and clearly what the book is about, the test is usually doomed. So here we tested *What Every Superintendent and Principal Needs to Know*. (Later we added "School Leadership for the Real World" as a subtitle, but after we had tested. That can be risky but on the cover and in subsequent flyer copy we kept the subtitle small and supportive.)

We arm-wrestled the Table of Contents into very simple, short units so that potential readers could quickly find subjects they wanted to know more about. And we put it in the prime real estate, top right, since we had no cover.

What Every
SUPERINTENDENT
and
PRINCIPAL
Needs to Know

Table of Contents

Finally, 256 pages of no-nonsense, usually funny, always honest ideas and techniques from three of Illinois' top administrators—for the price of a two-patty burger deal and a movie!

You will laugh from front to back but the book's intent is deadly serious: to propel you and your school or system straight to the top.

1. School Leadership
2. Civic Leadership
3. Business Leadership
4. Communications
5. Trust
6. Planning
7. Expert Knowledge
8. Building Internal Capacity for Success
9. Expanding District Boundaries
10. Supporting Successful Teaching and Learning
11. Adventures in Innovation
12. Taking Care of You

Why your board should buy this book for every administrator in your district—

The authors are three guys who rose to the top in school administration because, under fire, they could provide practical, successful solutions to almost any predicament. Even more, they could innovate, cut through the jargon and nonsense, and lead. So on these pages they share what they have learned: ideas, high-impact lessons about leadership, and everyday problem solving that can be immediately implemented at every school level. Their combined wisdom and stories will make administrators think, laugh, and act.

What Every
SUPERINTENDENT
and
PRINCIPAL
Needs to Know

A down-and-dirty guide to performing miracles, sidestepping mines, and emerging a happy, sane #1

Jim Rosborg, Ed.D.
Max McGee, Ph.D.
Jim Burgett, C.A.S.

Jim Rosborg
Superintendent of Belleville Public School District #118 in Belleville, Illinois, Jim received his Educational Doctorate from Southern Illinois University at Edwardsville and presently serves as an adjunct professor at St. Louis University, as President of the statewide Illinois Elementary District Organization, and serves on the Board of Directors for the Illinois Association of School Administrators.

Max McGee
Former Illinois State Superintendent of Education, Max currently serves as Superintendent of the Wilmette District #39. Max is a "lifer" in education with 30 years of experience and a Ph. D. from the University of Chicago.

Jim Burgett
During his 33-year tenure, Jim has served in almost every educational capacity. Named the Illinois Superintendent of the Year in 2001 and Administrator of the Year in 2002, Jim is currently the Superintendent of the Highland Community Unit School District and a nationally recognized educational speaker and presenter.

Paper trade, $19.95
6" x 9" / 256 pages
ISBN 0-910167-38-4
Available January, 2003
Details: www.sops.com

SATISFACTION GUARANTEED: If this book isn't *more* than we promise, send it back for a full refund, even if your dog chewed on it. No questions asked.

I patched together the form of a cover below the contents that, in reading after the fact, seems a bit flippant but does reflect the no-holds-barred nature of the text itself.

An issue was whether or not to use titles or degrees with the authors' names. Two had doctorates and all three had lots of extra letters they could tack on. We compromised in the test. I put them on the mock cover (we didn't use them on the actual book cover) but deleted them in the short biographies in the lower left corner, since doctorates were mentioned. There was no room for their photos on the flyer, nor any real purpose.

We added a SATISFACTION GUARANTEED on the test (and book), near the price, with a bit of fun included. (We've yet to have a book returned, incidentally, three years after its release. That is not uncommon in niche publishing. A 1% return rate to a niche market is very high, although the more you charge, the higher that rate might climb.)

Below the title, upper left, came the benefit text. We wanted the readers to know that there was plenty of fun, lots of practical advice, solutions, meat-and-bones stuff. So that's the core of the selling copy, with a "buy not one but many" plug in the box.

What's left is the important, bottom-line info: what does the book look like, how much does it cost, what does one get for that amount, and when will it be available? Add to that an ISBN number to show that this is a major book from a reputable publishing house (in deference, I guess, to a fast-copy hit-and-run item in wire binding from a sleazy huckster).

That appears bottom right below the cover. Remember, prices will differ so we can test various groups. (Only fliers sent to B and D will say $19.95.) To repeat, everything but the price on all of the fliers sent to the entire 500 will be precisely the same.

Incidentally, some of the details in the flyer are approximate. We guessed at 256 pages. It actually contains well over 300. I later changed the ISBN number. It actually came out in April, 2003. And we quickly created a different website to provide more information about the book and the authors. But it *is* a paper trade book and it does measure 6" x 9"!

If I had to measure the importance of the items tested, it would be: (1) title, (2) cover, (3) contents, (4) benefit copy, (5) authorship, and (6) cost and size. When it is paid for by a firm or institution, the cost is less important than the benefits, which might move up to second place.

Finally, there is no reason for the flyer to be multi-colored unless the cover is so spectacular that it is the strongest selling tool. One might use pastel or colored paper if that is consistent with the tone of the book, but black ink on white paper is probably the safest and certainly the least expensive.

I took all of the ideas the authors had sent me and condensed them into the test flyer that you see. That's not to say that there weren't small changes made, words switched, and (I'm sure, for the authors) breaths held, but ultimately they signed off on what you see in the test flyer.

Incidentally, one can always write sharper, more exact, better test fliers after the product itself appears. Not the least, you have a cover to add credence to the product. Some things can't be changed later, however, like the title and the contents—that's really what you are testing. (Or you must do a new test to see if they will buy the new title and contents.)

Last, the flyer must look professional, at least to the degree that there are no misspellings, everything is squared up, it is well balanced, and the content is accurate.

The Test Note

Once the flyer is done, a test note must be composed. These are one-third the size of an 8 ½" x 11" sheet of paper, or 3 2/3" high by 8 ½" wide. (Simply print three to a page, then cut that in thirds.) They fit in the #10 (business) envelope, unfolded, and are the first thing seen—and hopefully read!

As you can see in the test note that follows, this is a straight-forward request, in this case to a superintendent or principal, to look at the flyer accompanying the note, then respond (today!) by checking the appropriate boxes on the postcard.

It must be written in a tone that the recipient will find busi-nesslike yet friendly. A sprinkle of humor is acceptable as long as it is totally in context. Mostly, it must gently instruct them how to respond without attempting to overly influence their answer(s).

While there is a return address on the postcard, we also put an address here so the recipients can see that we are totally accessi-ble. (After I agreed to publish this book, I created an imprint [branch and publishing name] called Education Communication Unlimited. I suspect that if I had used that name as the return ad-dress on the note and postcard it might have generated more posi-tive responses, by indicating that we were in the education field.) The address is being changed here to correspond to our 2007 loca-tion(s).

TEST NOTE

Communication Unlimited / P.O. Box 845, Novato, CA 94948
(800) 563-1454 / fax (415) 883-5707
e-mail test@superintendents-and-principals.com

Dear Superintendent or Principal:

Would you do us a huge **30-second favor**? Read this note, skim the one-sided flyer enclosed, check the boxes on the postcard (it's not a test!), and mail or fax it back **today**?

Why? We need help! Three top school administrators in Illinois are finishing a book that we think will delight and significantly help every school administrator nationwide but we're uncertain both how to package it and whether folks like you are interested in buying this kind of information. So we are testing about three tenths of one percent (.3%) of top school administrators throughout the U.S. hoping they—you—will help us make it available in the best and least expensive manner, if desired. **How did you get so lucky** to be in that .3%? Maybe **brilliance**! Maybe bad luck.

Your response is totally anonymous, but please know that we are grateful for your help.

Gordon Schooler
C.E.O., Communication Unlimited

How do I know it will take 30 seconds? I don't, but it would take me 30 seconds. That's not where the war is at. It's in the anonymity, that they are a select group (.3%), and that we're asking for help in a positive way.

You'll note that rather than confuse them in the closing with the Burgett name (same as one of the authors), I use an historical family surname, Schooler. Only later did it dawn on me that for school administrators that name might have looked hokey or suspect. Oh, well, my Grandpa Okie liked it.

I ran the note by the authors and they gave it an okay.

The Postcard

What remains to complete the three-insert mailing packet is the postcard. This is an example of the postcard sent:

POSTCARD

I	[ ] would	buy *What Every Superintendent and Principal Needs to Know* for $19.95.
I	[ ] would not	
I	[ ] would	prefer to buy this book in a hard-cover edition costing $3 more.
I	[ ] would not	
I	[ ] would	prefer to buy this book in digital form, as an e-mail download, for $2 less, rather than bound.
I	[ ] would not	

Other thoughts I want to share:

Would you **fax**—(415) 883-5707—or **mail** this back today? Your help really is appreciated.

As I mentioned to the authors, I would cut card stock and put actual stamps on the cards since that increases the response rate significantly. On the mailing side, we carefully apply labels addressed to us, plus a stamp in the upper right corner.

What goes on the response side that I want the recipient to check? See the sample that follows.

Here we ask three questions: (1) Would you buy the book at _____ price? (2) Would you pay $3 more to buy it in hard cover form? (3) Would you pay $2 less as an e-mail digital download rather than receive the book in bound form?

Note that the response is almost effortless. It's yes or no in the first section (I would or wouldn't buy the book at that price), and only if interested, a check in the other sections too. And if they wish to share more about the idea, a place for that as well. Finally, a wee reminder on the bottom to please mail or fax it today. (I don't recall that anybody faxed it back.)

We don't want them to ponder this. We don't care why they'd buy it (or wouldn't) nor do we care if it should include more or less (hoping they might share that in the bottom section if their feelings are strong). Just a yes or no, with our thanks. Today!

The Mailing List

Let me share what we usually do regarding mailing lists, then how it differed here.

I would go to the library and find the *Standard Rate and Data Service Direct Mail Lists*, usually in the reference section. I'd spend an hour or two seeing all the ways this niche market might be served, then review the available lists, the brokers, the quantity of names listed, how they are compiled, how frequently they are cleaned, the cost, and anything else that seems relevant. From that I would copy the contact information from the top three lists, to pursue later from my office.

Let me share a few biases here. I prefer big rather than small in list providers (since they do it full time and the quality of their lists seems to be better). And I like list managers who are willing to work with me on finding the specific names that will serve me best. (It's good sense to contact other firms with products similar to yours using direct mail to see which lists and mangers they recommend.)

Then, as explained earlier, I like to test with 500 PS labels, nth selection in ZIP order. And I like to get that test list free, or at cost. The process is straightforward: I put my lists in preferred order and call the list manager of the first. I explain that we have a book about to be offered nationwide to school superintendents and principals. I plan to use the entire list at least once, probably more often. What I'd like to do is test it at various prices with 500 PS labels (nth selection in ZIP order). And, naturally, I'd like to do that free—that is, with free labels from your list—if possible, on the understanding (which I'll gladly put in writing) that if the test proves positive I will rent your list.

The list manager usually laughs, then asks some questions to make sure I'm not daft and that in fact such a book exists (I send him to the website to see what I have about it already posted). Then he says fine, give me a day or two—and when would you expect those results back (so he can call you soon after)? Or he will ask you to pay for the labels and shipping: $15 or $20. If he says no and talks about minimums ($100-250), courteously thank him, hang up, and try the second list, then the third, until you get a go-ahead or you have to swallow and pay the full minimum. (Once I did have to pay the full minimum; it's been about 50-50 between the free labels or paying modest costs the other times.)

Incidentally, there are list brokers who will find lists for you, act as an intermediary, and put it all in motion. They cost no more since they are paid through a discount given to them by the list company. But they don't like the free list business and sometimes their allegiance is more to the list provider than you, meaning you might be using inferior lists. They are in the *Yellow Pages*.

How did it work regarding our book, ***What Every Superintendent and Principal Needs to Know***?

I asked the authors early on, in passing, if they had access to superintendent or principal address lists. As it happened, one did, through an association. And since it was their money and simply a test to see if anybody would even buy such a heretical offering, I agreed to look at it, for possible use.

Clearly, I hadn't conveyed that properly because the next thing I knew I received full lists of superintendents in 10 x 3 format, but not from every state. In fact, many were from the smallest or Southern states, with Illinois and few other large states included.

So, with some reticence, I went ahead and used those names, even though that required a change in the postcard. Originally there was a fourth section on the response side that said: I am a [   ] superintendent [   ] principal [   ] _____. Since all on the list were superintendents, that section was deleted.

I used 462 names of superintendents in a two-step test. The first test I divided into two groups: 99 from Illinois and 93 nationwide (outside Illinois). To these groups I sent three equal price tests: $17.95, $19.95, and $24.95.

The second test used 270 names from outside Illinois. Because the highest response in both groups in the first test was at $19.95, I split the second list, 135 at $19.95 and 135 at $24.95.

Is it worth publishing?

The First Test Results

Let me simply share the information I sent to the authors about three weeks after the first test packets were mailed. (Most replies come in the first week, almost none after 20 days.)

> The first half of the test about your book for superintendents and principals is over. The results are very encouraging.

> First, not everybody will buy your book, so the best gauge (of who might) is a mail-out card like those I sent to each of you, with the flyer and short note. All we care about are those who mailed it back and checked yes. (About five sent back negative cards. Of course, all those not sent back were also negative cards!) A good response to a properly priced book is about 10%.

> Before the numbers, two uncertainties. It is very hard to nail down the number of superintendents. The best numbers I could get was 901 (45 regional/856 district) in Illinois and 16,836 (with mailing addresses we can contact) in the rest of the U.S., for a total of 17,737. The number of

school principals also varied but a mailing list I found had 3,583 in Illinois and 105,558 elsewhere, for 109,141 nationwide. So I used those numbers in my calculations.

The second was the very odd demography of the addresses we are using outside of Illinois, where almost all of the major states are deleted but the small and very rural states rule. Since the Illinois totals were higher than the national totals, and it is a more cosmopolitan, urbanized state than almost all of the others in our test, I suspect that the national numbers will be higher, perhaps considerably, if we had used a full-U.S. list.

Here are the totals for superintendents, which I'll interpret later:

ILLINOIS TOTALS / SUPTS				
Book Price	Postcards Sent	Positive Replies	%	Projected Sales
$17.95	33	3	9	81
$19.95	33	8	24	216
$24.95	33	6	18	162

NATIONAL TOTALS / SUPTS (minus Illinois)				
$17.95	31	4	13	2,189
$19.95	31	7	23	3,872
$24.95	31	3	10	1,684

Since we did not mail to principals, the best we can do is guess. I am guessing about a 10% buy ratio, which I suspect is low, for any priced book that we sell. If there are a total of 109,148 principals, that would increase the sales by 10,915 books.

Using those totals, what kind of income might your book expect to bring? Let's eliminate the $17.95 price since it was the least sought and focus on $19.95 and $24.95.

POSSIBLE GROSS INCOME				
Source	Buy %	Total Buyers	$ 19.95	$ 24.95
Supts, Ilinois	17%	901	$ 3,052	$ 3,817
Principals, Illinois	10%	3,590	7,162	8,957
Supts, US	15%	16,835	50,379	63,005
Principals, US	10%	105,558	210,588	263,367
Totals		$ 126,884	$ 271,181	$ 339,146

The "buy %" above is a conservative estimate based on the first test.

Incidentally, it was good that we tested the other two means since we know that neither will significantly increase the potential earnings. To the question, "Would the person buy this book in a hard-cover edition costing $3 more, five in Illinois and five nationwide (of 192, or 5.2%) said yes. To the second question, "Would they prefer to buy the book in digital form, as an e-mail download, for $2 less, no superintendent in Illinois said yes and only three did nationwide. At first look, neither seems to be worth the cost of producing, on the assumption that they would buy it anyway in the standard form if the alternative didn't exist.

What does that mean to you three gents?

Let's say the book brought in a $300,000 direct-mail response, which is what the numbers from the first mailing indicate (if the 10% buy rate from principals is accurate). It might, over the life of the book, double that (if additional books are diligently sold other ways), but a more prudent guess would be $450,000 gross, if the book has a long shelf life.

If you plan to pool your brilliance and self-publish it, you could expect about 25% in profit over the long haul, which would be $25,000 each from the direct-mail income and another $12,500 each later, or $37,500 apiece, plus, of course, the fame and free cigars of authorship.

If you went to a standard publisher, the absolute maximum you would get is 12% divided by three, but much more likely an 8.5-10% total, again divided by three. Figuring 12%, that would be $12,000 each from the first rush, with another $6,000 later, or $18,000.

Good news. Tomorrow we will prepare postcards and fliers for the rest of the list, to see their response to the $19.95 and $24.95 price levels. (It makes no sense to test $22.95 or so because book buyers usually think in multiples of $5).

The Second Test

The second test, as mentioned, used recipients outside of Illinois, 135 tested at $19.95 and the same number at $24.95. After three weeks, the results were as follows:

NATIONAL TOTALS / SUPTS (minus Illinois)				
Book Price	Postcards Sent	Positive Replies	%	Projected Sales
$19.95	135	10	7.41	1,248
$24.95	135	12	8.89	1,497

That would make the entire test results as follows:

ILLINOIS TOTALS / SUPTS (Test 1 only)				
Book Price	Postcards Sent	Positive Replies	%	Projected Sales
$17.95	33	3	9	81
$19.95	33	8	24	216
$24.95	33	6	18	162

NATIONAL TOTALS / SUPTS (minus Illinois, both tests)				
$17.95	31	4	13	2,189
$19.95	166	17	10.24	1,816
$24.95	166	15	9.04	1,603

POSSIBLE GROSS INCOME					
Source	Buy %	Buyers / $ at $ 19.95		Buyers / $ at $24.95	
Supts, Ilinois	18-24%	216	$ 4,309	162	$4,042
Principals, Illinois	10%	350	7,142	358	8,932
Supts, US	9-10%	1,724	34,394	1,522	37,974
Principals, US	10%	10,559	210,652	10,559	263,448
Totals		12,857	$ 256,497	12,601	$ 314,396

A summary of the tests, then, would suggest that the most profitable price is $24.95—it begs the question of a second test at $29.95 and $34.95. It shows a tested result of $42,016 could be expected from a short run of some 2,000 books if confined only to superintendents. (If the authors/publisher decided to limit it to superintendents, another test should indeed be done with that only in the title. The tighter the focus market in the title, the higher one might expect the return to be from the selected, tested recipients.)

On the other hand, while the 10% selling ratio to principals is untested in this field (though common in niche-marketed books), by combining the two markets (superintendents and principals), the potential additional income (at 10%) would be $272,380 (at $24.95) for principals and $42,016 for superintendents, or $314,396 total. That presumes a book run of some 13,000 books.

This then begs two quick calculations. One for the authors: how much might they earn in self-publishing income if the sales equal the tested results and 10% estimate, and (for me) how profitable would it be for my firm to take all of the risk and assume all of the preparation and marketing costs (see Post Test Decisions)?

Let's use $300,000 as the direct-mail income response, to be conservative. Then the numbers don't change much from what I suggested in the response to the first test. Should they self-publish, they might expect, at most, $25,000 each from direct-mail sales and $12,500 from ancillary sales, or $37,500 each. But somebody must do the publishing work, and unless all three do a third at no cost, those totals will be nibbled away.

Comments by Test Recipients

Sometimes the bottom half of the postcard also brings solid suggestions or sales leads, though almost all leave it blank. What did our 462 respondents say? Not much, frankly.

Twelve wrote comments. Seven simply gave us their name and address, which earned them a mailed flyer/order form as soon as it existed, plus a thank-you note for having responded! Two of the seven said "Sounds very good!" and "Sounds like a great book." Another sent regards to one of the authors.

Two addressed the download possibility, one asking, "If in digital form, what would the recopy limits be?"—but gave no return address. The other said, "The download option is a good idea. I would probably buy the book anyway!"

Another wished us "Good luck." While the last two offered specific assistance:

The first: "Particular interest in chapters 1, 2, 6, 7, 8, 10, and 12."

The second: "You are on to something if you can make it quick, real, funny, and useful. Remember, most of us simply will not sit still long enough to read a book cover to cover. We'll pick it up and 'skim.'"

Post-Test Decisions

It was fairly clear to me that none of the three authors had the time or inclination to undertake the publishing of this book. They are at the peak of their careers, extraordinarily successful, in demand to speak widely while then still serving as superintendents in large districts, and all are, properly, well compensated. And the book interested me since it fit firmly in my area of niche publishing.

So I proposed to them that, if interested, I would be delighted to publish this book (a gamble since I'd yet to see much of their writing) and would pay them each 5% of the net income, or 15% total. In exchange, I'd do (or pay for) the editing, proofing, cover prep, artwork, typesetting, layout, printing, shipping, and marketing. The rest of the details were standard fare for nonfiction books, though they could buy the books directly from us at 40% off (plus shipping) for any back-of-the-room or other sales that didn't directly compete with our direct mail or library sales.

What numbers was I using to calculate my profitability as a publisher?

I figured the production cost of the book at about $3.75, including shipping from the printer and the shrink wrapping of each book.

The initial 85-90% of the marketing would be by direct mail. For that I calculated about 42 cents a flyer (almost all for mailing list rental, postage, flyer design and printing, and flyer shipping from the printer to the mailing house). Since the selling ratio according to the tests would be about 1:10, a sale would cost me $4.20 plus $3.75 for production, or $7.95 each. Say $8 a book sold by mail. Add to that another $1 for fulfillment and $1 more for overhead and incidentals and the book will cost me $10 for a $24.95 sale. Then subtract $3.75 for royalties (a third to each author), and my profit for mail order sales would be approximately $11.20 a book, or 45%. Not a windfall, but enough.

Let me quickly add what other factors influenced my decision:

(1) All three are excellent speakers, in high demand, and there should be strong back-of-the-room sales of their books, by themselves or the sponsoring organizations.

(2) We will vigorously pursue other selling venues, in addition to direct mail, like actual and digital bookstore sales, college textbook selection, college library sales, association book lists, sponsored reward programs using the book as a prize or gift, distributors in the academic field, and appearance book signings by the authors.

(3) A website has been created to help potential buyers and users learn more about the book, the authors, and the topics that the book develops. It will be the core of a public relations program designed to share articles, news releases, and radio/TV appearances from the authors or the publishing firm, and to make subsequent products available (and fully explained) to buyers.

(4) We propose to follow up the release of the book with a series of specific reports written, hopefully, by each of the authors (and others) that expand in far greater detail many of the items touched upon in the book, plus other reports that subsequent academic activities suggest. (Seen from 2007, this never materialized. Too labor intensive for the potential returns.)

The authors considered the proposal and appropriately asked for more details. I provided answers to any questions they had, sent a contract for their reading, and soon thereafter the book became the publishing challenge of the then new imprint, Education Communication Unlimited.

Gathering information and writing the book

What followed was the usual book preparation stuff. We set up deadlines and rough chapter lengths, and I left it to the three to iron out the composition details among themselves, on the understanding that it adhere fairly closely to the tested promises in the flyer's Table of Contents.

Chapters were sent to me by e-mail. All three were solid writers, had a sense of humor, and provided well researched text. Alas, 30-some years in academia produced fairly stodgy, cautious prose. My background is in newspaper and magazine writing, a different cat. So, to their horror, I boiled away the jargon, cut the sentences in half, reduced paragraph length, and lightened the structure even more, so the book would be "fun" to read and enlightening at the same time. Fortunately, all caught the spirit of the leavening, and when they received their copy back, well dotted with red, they dug in, rewrote, modified, expanded, or contracted their offerings. It took about six months until a dandy book was hammered into shape. At last, the whole book was edited and proofed, a designer created the cover, and it was sent off to a printer. What made it work was that all three authors were used to stress, were deadline-keepers, and they all knew their topics and were articulate about them. So it was a felicitous union of four hard workers all with the same goal—creating an excellent book that would surpass our test's promises.

Using P.O.D. printing?

There was no thought of using print-on-demand here since the quantities needed were in the thousands and the quality and price of web press printing made it the logical conclusion. Had I wanted 50 or even 100 early copies to use for some pre-marketing, that would have been a sensible alternative, with web press printing the follow-up for larger quantities.

Promoting and selling the book

This is still an active book. An updated, revised version of the **What Every Superintendent and Principal Needs to Know**, with the same basic contents, was released in mid-2007 at the same price. Several months later we released a second book by the same three authors called **The Perfect School** (also at $24.95), and at the end of 2007 my firm published **Teachers Change Lives 24/7** by brother Jim, at $17.95.

That was done for two reasons: (1) because of the financial [selling] success of the first book and the interest generated in what else the three authors had to say about school direction and (2) in the TCE tradition, it is easier and more profitable to expand from the original base and sell more, related, solid products.

The mixing of products, however, muddies the monetary waters as to what amount or percentage of the gross come from which book, particularly when they are bundled and sold two or three at a discount.

So final income numbers and sales for our target book are still impossible to share, although the actual marketing process before the additional books isn't.

The initial direct mail campaign

Before the book was finished I began my direct mail marketing plan. I studied the available mailing lists to school superintendents and principals and selected MCH, which had 13,977 superintendents of city and county school systems, 1,430 County Superintendents of Schools, and 447 church-related and Catholic school superintendents. (We decided not to mail to Canada because of its small market, the high shipping expense, and the handling barriers.) So our first flyer mailing was to 15,854 superintendents, costing 4 cents a name. This was quite successful.

I then planned to mail five more times to principals in lots of about 25,000 each, at 3 cents a name, to (1) senior high principals (public, Catholic, and private), totaling 25,597; to both K-12 and middle/junior high principals, 12,711 and 15,850 respectively, for a total of 28,561; (3) the elementary principals, totaling 82,331, or about 27,450 in each of three different mailings. The mailing to principals was contingent upon the response in the first two mailings. They would be done in that order, the first two before the holidays in 2003, the last four between January and late April of 2004. This wasn't as successful. My estimate of a 10% response was much higher than the reality—not fatal, since the returns at about 4% for the first two mailings brought profits nonetheless.

But it shows the folly of not adhering strictly to my original test pattern of mailing to both superintendents and principals. We stopped the mailing to principals after two attempts.

The First Direct Mail Flyer

What follows are both sides of our direct mail flyer. Check both out at www.superintendents-and-principals.com/flyer2.htm. and www.superintendents-and-principals.com/flyer3.htm) where they are larger and in color!

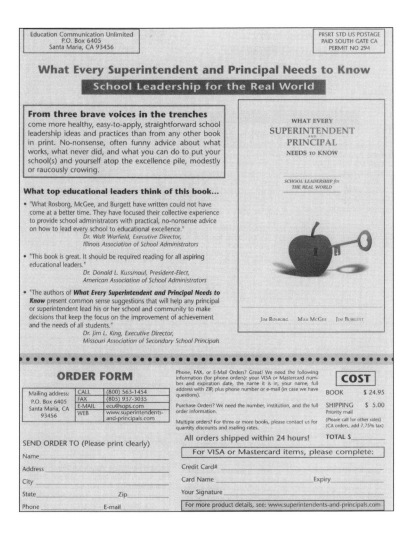

What Every Superintendent and Principal Needs to Know

School Leadership for the Real World

From three brave voices in the trenches

come more healthy, easy-to-apply, straightforward school leadership ideas and practices than from any other book in print. No-nonsense, often funny advice about what works, what never did, and what you can do to put your school(s) and yourself atop the excellence pile, modestly or raucously crowing.

What top educational leaders think of this book...

- "What Rosborg, McGee, and Burgett have written could not have come at a better time. They have focused their collective experience to provide school administrators with practical, no-nonsense advice on how to lead every school to educational excellence."
  Dr. Walt Warfield, Executive Director,
  Illinois Association of School Administrators

- "This book is great. It should be required reading for all aspiring educational leaders."
  Dr. Donald L. Kussmaul, President-Elect,
  American Association of School Administrators

- "The authors of **What Every Superintendent and Principal Needs to Know** present common sense suggestions that will help any principal or superintendent lead his or her school and community to make decisions that keep the focus on the improvement of achievement and the needs of all students."
  Dr. Jim L. King, Executive Director,
  Missouri Association of Secondary School Principals

WHAT EVERY
SUPERINTENDENT
AND
PRINCIPAL
NEEDS TO KNOW

SCHOOL LEADERSHIP for
THE REAL WORLD

JIM ROSBORG   MAX McGEE   JIM BURGETT

ORDER FORM

Phone, FAX, or E-Mail Orders? Great! We need the following information (for phone orders): your VISA or Mastercard number and expiration date, the name it is in, your name, full address with ZIP, plus phone number or e-mail (in case we have questions).

Purchase Orders? We need the number, institution, and the full order information.

Multiple orders? For three or more books, please contact us for quantity discounts and mailing rates.

Mailing address:	CALL	(800) 563-1454
P.O. Box 6405	FAX	(805) 937-3035
Santa Maria, CA	E-MAIL	ecu@sops.com
93456	WEB	www.superintendents-and-principals.com

All orders shipped within 24 hours!

COST

BOOK $ 24.95

SHIPPING $ 5.00
Priority mail
(Please call for other rates)
(CA orders, add 7.75% tax)

TOTAL $_____

SEND ORDER TO (Please print clearly)

Name_____

Address_____

City_____

State_____ Zip_____

Phone_____ E-mail_____

For VISA or Mastercard items, please complete:

Credit Card#_____

Card Name_____ Expiry_____

Your Signature_____

For more product details, see: www.superintendents-and-principals.com

What Every
SUPERINTENDENT
and
PRINCIPAL
Needs to Know

School Leadership for the Real World

"The Buck Stops With Us!"

Modestly stated, this book shares more sound, straightforward, easy-to-apply school leadership ideas and practices than any other book in print. Three of Illinois' top educational leaders offer 336 pages of no-nonsense, often funny advice about what works and what doesn't, ranging from assessment to personal hygiene to getting those irksome referenda passed to what to say to the press, and when. It's simply a must for every school administrator.

Why your Board should buy this book for every administrator in your district—

The authors are three guys who rose to the top in school administration because, under fire, they could provide practical, successful solutions to almost any predicament. Even more, they could innovate, cut through the jargon and nonsense, and lead. So on these pages, they share what they have learned: ideas, high-impact lessons about leadership, and everyday problem solving that can be immediately implemented at every school level. Their combined wisdom and stories will make administrators think, laugh, and act.

Jim Rosborg
Superintendent of Belleville Public School District #118 in Belleville, Illinois, Jim received his Educational Doctorate from Southern Illinois University at Edwardsville and presently serves as an adjunct professor at St. Louis University, as President of the statewide Illinois Elementary District Organization, and on the Board of Directors for the Illinois Association of School Administrators.

Max McGee
Former Illinois State Superintendent of Education, Max currently serves as Superintendent of Wilmette School District #39. Max is a "lifer" in education with 30 years of experience and a Ph. D. from the University of Chicago.

Jim Burgett
During his 33-year tenure, Jim has served in almost every educational capacity. Named the Illinois Superintendent of the Year in 2001 and Administrator of the Year in 2002, Jim is currently Superintendent of the Highland Community Unit School District and a nationally recognized educational speaker and presenter.

Table of Contents

1. School Leadership
2. Civic Leadership and Ethics
3. Business Basics for School Leaders
4. Communications
5. Building and Sustaining Trust
6. Planning
7. Expert Knowledge
8. Building Internal Capacity
9. Visionary Leadership
10. Successful Teaching and Learning
11. Adventures in Innovation
12. Taking Care of YOU!
13. Standards, Assessment, and Accountability
14. Case Studies in Real-World Leadership

Paper trade, $24.95
6" x 9" / 336 pages
ISBN 0-9708621-6-4

Details: www.superintendents-and-principals.com

SATISFACTION GUARANTEED: If this book isn't more than we promise, send it back for a full refund, even if your dog chewed on it. No questions asked.

Since the first flyer was directed to superintendents, I asked the authors to please contact friends and colleagues in high places who were respected to see if we could get some initial testimonials to be put on the flyer. We sent galley copies of the text to those who seemed interested, and got three resounding testimonials under "What top educational leaders think of this book…" (You can see them on the flyer and at the website under "testimonials.")

I also had the website fully functioning, created the imprint (Education Communication Unlimited), and developed the email address (no longer ours) referred to in the flyer. The rest was updated information from the test flyer, but in red, yellow, and black on white. The printing bid for this flyer (and the second) went to Tu-Vets Corp. in Los Angeles, and we used their indicia (thus the South Gate) in the bulk mailing.

The second direct mail flyer

Since all subsequent direct mail fliers would be directed to school principals, I prevailed on the authors to again ask principals and their associations for flyer testimonials from school leaders who had read the book. That produced 15 from which I selected six (and put the rest on the website) for the second flyer.

I also needed to make changes between the first and second flyer. The Table of Contents side was left the same, with one exception: I moved the book details to the other side and replaced them, under the Table of Contents and above the website address, with the question

"Want to read the full Chapter 1,
more about the Table of Contents,
and what others think of this book?

As you can see in the flyer that follows (also visible in color at www.superintendents-and-principals.com/flyer4.htm), I prefer a full one-third address panel, so the top third is just that, with copy rewritten and refitted. The center panel (or third) includes the six testimonials from the principals. The book particulars appear in a box in the center of that panel, plus new copy again directing them to the website. The bottom panel, the order form, is the same.

Other marketing means

While direct mail provided most of the sales, the most profitable means of income-generation were at conferences or conventions of the superintendent-related associations, usually when one or all of the authors participated, and by the authors themselves as BOR items or to participants at their workshops and academies as part of the registration fee.

The website draws lots of visitors and they remain a surprisingly long time, thus a few orders trickle down through the order form. We sold to most of the education-based libraries and modestly to university holdings, but those are one-time sales and, in this case, small. The book was well reviewed in peer publications (almost all the association newsletters) but that mostly got the authors booked to speak, with book sales coming later.

Small publishers have difficulty getting a wholesaler or distributor, which in turn makes sales to major bookstores virtually impossible. Only as this book is being written (in late 2007), with three education books approved by Barnes and Noble, was my firm able to arrange the wholesaler to place the orders. Even that will not make much of a dent in the net income, nor will the occasional book sold through Amazon.com.

What will affect sales (and where we have been slow to take the initiative) is with articles linked to the contents of the book, as reprints or updated rewrites. The bio slug is an excellent selling tool, where the author is identified, achievements and books written are listed, and the website noted, for further information. If the article is good, the reader wants more—and superintendents and principals are, usually, avid readers.

Another asset is that, while the education field is always in flux, books about the verities and how to manage and dominate those changes have long shelf lives. The hardest thing is to put those books before the leaders' eyes regularly with follow-up contact information.

Converting the book into more books

We have approached this add-on and building concept in three ways.

One, we created an updated, revised edition in 2007, a bit over three years later. I approached each of the authors and asked if there was enough change to warrant an update, and would they perform that magic on their 4 1/3 chapters. They said yes to the latter, and "some change but not a lot" to the former. So I put out the call, we added and subtracted from the case studies, three chapters were rewritten, there were a few modifications in the others, and verb tenses were changed since all three of the authors were in different positions by 2007.

What resulted was a tighter, more up-to-date book, but one that was really about 90% the same. Too few changes to go back to the first buyers urging them to get #2 and too few and scattered to create an updated "booklet" to sell at a modest price, yet new enough to get an honest 2007 copyright, a new selling life, and part of a two- or three-book series at the on-site sales.

Two, instead of revamping the first book entirely (if that could even be done), we asked a different question, "If one could start with a clean slate, how would they create *The Perfect School*? What would it look like? How does one's school now compare to that?"

We divided that model into the respective authors' three areas of specialization, I wrote the introduction and opening chapter addressing the concept of "perfection" in education and why we even suggested it, and the result became a partner to the first book and a new speaking topic to be shared with their peers, with the actual books, again, as BOR products. Further, since many graduate education classes had adopted the first book as a textbook, it opened up the possibility of additional inclusion of the second book in academic curricula.

Which is a roundabout way of saying we now have two sister books that will each help sell the other, and with two books it is sensible to return again to the direct mail route to sell one, the other, or both.

The third way builds on the second. With Jim Burgett concurrently writing *Teachers Change Lives 24/7*, and speaking widely about the theme, and with us publishing all three books (and all seeing light in 2007), it gives us an even stronger reason for developing a new flyer with three valuable education tools and putting that flyer in every education leader's mail.

(As this book is going to press, that three-book flyer is being received by 14,400 superintendents across the country. A $6,000 gamble. But if only 1% buy our three-book offer at $50 [an $18 reduction, as a leader] we will be $1,000 in the black. And if 5%

do, as we anticipate, that will bring in $30,000. Subtracting $6 a book for production and related costs, that's a profit of $23,040. And we suspect that many [perhaps 100] will later buy one, two, or even all three books in larger quantities for use with study groups or associations. Not much of a gamble at all.)

Sharing the book's information by other dissemination means?

If the authors of *What Every Superintendent and Principal Needs to Know* weren't still extremely busy, perhaps other venues might be explored. The book already exists digitally and its use in chapter form was tried without much interest shown. The next logical step is to build an audio CD version of the book for those more interested in hearing than reading it. But I'm not entertaining that venue because audio CDs are hard to sell, take lots of time to do right, and the responses from those to whom I sporadically asked if they would rather hear than read the book were uniformly negative.

So this book will have to stand on its own in the future, with spin-off help from the other two books, the new direct mail just sent, its occasional appearance in bookstores, and the vigorous speaking campaigns of its authors. Of course, there's always the remote chance that the readers of *Niche Publishing* might also have an uncle or sister leading the educational wars in dire need of the book's valuable (and fun) contents!

**"If you have knowledge, let others
light their candles at it."**

Margaret Fuller (1810-50)

OTHER SOURCES AND GUIDES

The best books I know about this subject

There are two books that are invaluable for the new book creator. They fully describe, step-by-step, the mechanics of the self-publishing process:

Dan Poynter, *The Self-Publishing Manual* (Para Publishing, 15th rev. ed., 2006), $19.95
Tom and Marilyn Ross, *The Complete Guide to Self-Publishing* (Writer's Digest Books, 4th ed., 2002), $19.99.

Alas, they do not focus on niche market publishing but rather on how the self-publisher can do (often better) what larger publishers do for general markets. I highly recommended either for information about book production and general book promotion.

An older book but an eye-opener about publishing in general:

Judith Appelbaum, *How to Get Happily Published: A Complete and Candid Guide* (HarperCollins, 5th ed., 1998) $15.95.

It's almost always necessary to hire out for services to make your book a reality. Sometimes this is done informally. Other times explicit written contracts are more appropriate. An inexpensive way to prepare needed contracts is to select from 22 model contracts on disc, download what you need, modify them with the numbers appropriate to your situation, make the slight alterations required, and print out (in Word or PDF) your own agreement(s) ready for signature. For years I've used:

Dan Poynter and Charles Kent, *Publishing Contracts* (Para Publishing), $29.95.

I also like another book that discusses the law and writing quite well:

Leonard DuBoff and Bert Krages, *The Law (in Plain English) for Writers*, (Sourcebooks, 4th ed., 2005), $16.95.

Although niche marketing focuses on the niche, there are many ways of reaching that niche. So a solid grasp of direct marketing in general is essential for one's empire to grow and expand. I like these books:

John Kremer, *1001 Ways to Markets Your Books* (Open Horizons, 6th rev. ed., 2006), $27.95.

David Cole, *The Complete Guide to Book Marketing*, (Allworth Press, 2nd rev. ed., 2004), $19.95.

Bob Stone and Ron Jacobs, *Successful Direct Marketing Methods* (McGraw-Hill, 8th ed, 2007), $59.95.

Roddy Mullin, *Direct Marketing* (Kogan Page, Ltd, 2002), $22.95.

Seth Godin, *Permission Marketing: Turning Strangers Into Friends, and Friends into Customers* (Simon & Schuster, 1999), $25.

The two books most directly related to niche publishing are mine, though both are now dated. This book lays the base of how one thinks and plans an empire. The concepts it contains are still valid and usable.

Gordon Burgett, *Empire-Building by Writing and Speaking* (Communication Unlimited, 1987), $12.95.

After outlining the many means of information dissemination one can use to create an empire, I wrote the following book to give the how-to details needed to implement them. The costs today read like a Sears & Roebuck catalog of 1905 and a few of the means have all but disappeared, but the format used can still be applied. This book is scheduled for updating in 2008.

Gordon Burgett, *Niche Marketing for Writers, Speakers, and Entrepreneurs* (Communication Unlimited, 1993), $14.95.

The best book of all about writing is in its 30th year. Every writer should be forced to read:

William Zinsser, *On Writing Well*, (Collins, 9th ed., 2006), $14.95.

What about the topic of niching? I so like Chris Andserson's book on where it is today and, by extension, where it will be as the digital world continues to explode that I added Chapter 18 to discuss it after this book was set to print!

Chris Anderson, *The Long Tail: Why the Future of Business Is Selling Less of More* (Hyperion, 2006), $24.95.

There are other good books available that approach the topic soundly:

Lynda Falkenstein, *Nichecraft, Using Your Specialness to Focus Your Business, Corner Your Market and Make Customers Seek You Out*, (Niche Press, 2nd ed., 2000), $24.95.

W. Chan Kim, *Blue Ocean Strategy: How to Create Uncontested Market Space and Make the Competition Irrelevant* (Harvard University, 2005), $ 29.95.

Michael Treacy and Fred Wiersema, *The Discipline of Market Leaders: Choose Your Customer, Narrow Your Focus, Dominate Your Market* (Perseus Books Group, 1997), $ 15.

Jennifer Basye Sander and Peter Sander, *Niche and Grow Rich* (Entrepreneur Press, 2003), $ 16.95.

Not all niche publishers limit their scope as tightly as I have shown in this book. For those with broader niches (like men, women, seniors, kids), they must often use the standard publishing techniques of general market books. That's where the books by Poynter, Ross, and Kremer are particularly useful, as are the books that follow:

Robert Lee Brown and Chuck Sambuchino, *Writer's Market 2008*, (Writer's Digest Books, 2007), $29.99.

Jeff Herman, *Jeff Herman's Guide to Publications, Editors, and Literary Agents—2008* (3 Dog Press, 2007), $29.95.

Michael Larsen, *How to Write a Book Proposal*, (Writer's Digest Books, 3rd ed., 2004), $15.99.

Jeff Herman and Deborah Levine Herman, *Write the Perfect Book Proposal: 10 That Sold and Why*, (Wiley, 2nd ed, 2001), $15.95.

Cynthia Laufenberg, *Formatting and Submitting Your Manuscript*, (Writer's Digest Books, 2nd ed, 2004), $19.99.

Aaron Shepard, *Perfect Pages: Self Publishing with Microsoft Word, or How to Avoid High-Priced Page Layout Programs or Book Design Fees and Produce Fine Books in MS Word for Desktop Publishing and Print on Demand*, (Shepard Publications, 2006), $16.

INDEX

HOW TO SET UP AND MARKET YOUR OWN SEMINAR

Gordon Burgett

Seminars are an excellent way to establish your expertise, get it and you widely known, and earn you a handsome lifelong return from helping others.

In the niche field, seminars and books are the two best ways to prove to others that you know your stuff. From that, empires are built!

What can you share that others would eagerly pay to know? What do you know that can make others richer, happier, healthier, or more secure, stimulated, or satisfied?

Identify a way to meet others' needs, expand your knowledge, organize a presentation, and you have the main elements of a seminar or workshop. Give it and you will be part of a multibillion dollar industry still in its infancy.

This new audio CD series tells you how to get started, find a topic, locate markets and sponsors, determine price, replace risk with profit, register, promote, advertise, and much more. The 31-page workbook (including an indispensable organizational calendar) is worth the price of the program alone!

For 20+ years, Gordon was one of the most prolific seminar-givers in America (he still offers about 40 annually), with 2,000+ programs and many thousands of followers.

When he was asked so often how he set up his seminars and how they could do the same—at colleges, to associations or businesses, or to the public at large,—he researched the entire topic, interviewed other successful seminar-givers, wrote a book about it, and—huge surprise!—created a new seminar.

The book, *Speaking for Money*, has been out of print for about a decade, but Gordon's popular seminar has been updated annually and is now available in this four-disc audio CD program.

3 audio **CD discs**
(50 minutes @)
and a fourth disc with
the full **workbook**,
downloadable.

$45 plus shipping
and tax (in CA)

What does Gordon speak about on the audio CDs?

Brief introduction
Overview of seminars and their income fonts
Eight kinds of seminars
Defining and choosing between public institutional, private busi-
    ness/corporate, and public self-sponsored seminars
How do you find a subject?
An organizational guideline
Feasibility study: how you learn from others
Writing a description and creating a title
Identifying the market most likely to pay to attend your program
Selecting the most appropriate sponsor....or doing it yourself
Creating workbooks and making back-of-the-room sales
Booking / Price / Time / Location / Promotion
A summary and a call to action!

To order this or any other product from
Communication Unlimited, please see

PRODUCTS WE SELL

BOOKS	Digital Price	Print Price
Niche Publishing (2008)	$16.95	$19.95
Niche Marketing for Writers and Speakers		14.95
Empire-Building by Writing and Speaking		12.95
Travel Writer's Guide (3rd ed.)	15.95	17.95
How to Plan a Great Second Life (2nd ed.)	15.95	17.95
Treasure and Scavenger Hunts (3rd ed.)	15.95	17.95
Lian McAndrews / Perfect Human World (novel)	5.00	

AUDIO CDs	Audio CD
How To Set Up and Market Your Own Seminar (includes downloadable workbook)	45
Testing a Niche Book Before Writing It	15
Creating Your Own Audio CDs	15
How to Sell 75% of Your Travel Writing (includes downloadable workbook)	30
How to Plan a Great Second Life	10

WRITING REPORTS		
101 Business Tips: Writers and Small Publishers	10	12
25 Professional Query and Cover Letters	10	12
Finding Topics for General and Travel Articles	10	12

NICHE PUBLISHING REPORTS		
100 Niche Marketing Topics	12	14
Creating Your Own Audio CDs	13	15

BOOKS FOR EDUCATORS		
What Every Superintendent and Principal Needs to Know (2nd ed.) by Rosborg, McGee, Jim Burgett	20	24.95
The Perfect School by Rosborg, McGee, J. Burgett	20	24.95
Teachers Change Lives 24/7 (2nd ed.) by Jim Burgett	14	17.95

For details about all of the items listed above, including shipping, tax, and bulk discounts, call (800) 563-1454 or please see the **ORDER FORM** at www.gordonburgett.com/order3.htm.